THE

ROMAN SURVEYORS

IN

CUMBERLAND

Ditch and agger at Sockbridge Hall that R.G. Collingwood believed to be a remnant of High Street, en route to Brougham Roman fort. It coincides with cadaster B *limes* K 44. The ditch has been preserved in the modern field drainage system.

THE
ROMAN SURVEYORS
IN
CUMBERLAND

By

Alan Richardson

THE ROMAN SURVEYORS

IN

CUMBERLAND

Alan Richardson

Copyright © 2008 Alan Richardson

The right of Alan Richardson to be identified as the Author of this Work has been asserted by him in accordance with the Copyright, Designs and Patents Act 1988.

ISBN-10-09547739-9-3
ISBN-13 978-0-9547739-9-1

Apart from any use permitted under UK copyright law, this publication may only be reproduced, stored, or transmitted, in any form, or by any means, with prior permission in writing of the publisher or, in the case of reprographic production, in accordance with the terms of licences issued by the Copyright Licensing Agency.

First Published in Great Britain
in January 2008 by P3 Publications,
13 Beaver Road,
Carlisle,
Cumbria, CA2 7PS
www.p3publications.com

Typeset in Times Roman
Printed and bound in Great Britain by
Amadeus Press
Cleckheaton
BD19 4TQ

CONTENTS

	Preface	vii
1.	The Romans in East Cumberland	1
2.	A Roman survey in East Cumberland	9
3.	The Roman survey of Britain	27
4.	Cumberland revisited	33
5.	Evidence of other Roman roads and cadasters	47
6.	Appendices	59
7	Bibliography	67
8.	Index	71

ARCHAEOLOGICAL PUBLICATION BY THE AUTHOR

1. Richardson A., 1983: *Evidence of Centuriation in the Inglewood Forest,* Trans. C&WAAS, (2nd Series) LXXXII, 67-71.
2. Richardson A., 1982: *Evidence of Centuriation at Manchester*, Cheshire Archaeological Bulletin, Vol. 9, 9-17.
3. Richardson A., 1984: *An Old Road in the Eden Valley,* Trans. C&WAAS, (2nd Series), LXXXIV, 79-83.
4. Richardson A., 1986: *Further evidence of Centuriation in Cumbria,* Trans. C&WAAS, 2nd Series, LXXXVI, 71-78.
5. Richardson A., 1986: Further evidence of Centuriation at Manchester, The Manchester Geographer, (NS) 7, 44-51.
6. Richardson A., 1987: *Some Evidence of Early Roman Military Activity on the South West Pennine Flank, The Reginald Taylor Prize Essay* for 1985, J. Brit. Arch. Ass'n., CXL, 18-35.
7. Richardson A. and Allan T.M., 1990: *The Roman Road over the Kirkstone Pass: Ambleside to Old Penrith*, Trans. C&WAAS, 2nd Series, XC, 105-125.
8. Richardson A. and Allan T.M., 1992: *Enclosures on Brackenrigg,* Trans. C&WAAS, 2nd Series, XCII, 273-274.
9. Richardson A., 1997: *Observations on the Geometry of Roman Camps,* Trans. C&WAAS, 2nd Series, XCVII, 45-55.
10. Richardson A., 2000: *The Numerical Basis of Roman Camps,* Oxford Journal of Archaeology, *Vol. 19, No 4, 425-437.*
11. Richardson A., 2001: *The Order of Battle in the Roman Army: Evidence from marching camps,* Oxford Journal of Archaeology, Vol. 20, No 2, 171-185.
12. Richardson A., 2002: *Camps and forts of units and formations of the Roman Army,* Oxford Journal of Archaeology, Vol. 21, No 1, 93-107.
13. Richardson A., 2002:*Some probable Roman roads in east Cumbria,* Trans. C&WAAS, 3rd Series, II, 307-310.
14. Ferrar M.J. & Richardson A., 2003: *The Roman Survey of Britain,* British Archaeological Reports, British Series 359, Oxford.
15. Richardson A., 2002: *Space and manpower in Roman camps*, Oxford Journal of Archaeology, Vol. 22, No 3, 303-313.
16. Richardson A., 2003: *The possible historic contexts of some Roman camps in Cumberland,* Trans. C&WAAS, 3rd Series, III, 91-95.
17. Ferrar M.J. & Richardson A., 2004: L'Arpentage Romain de la Grande-Bretagne, Archeologie, No 408.
18. Richardson A., 2004: *Granaries and Garrisons in Roman Forts,* Oxford Journal of Archaeology, Vol. 23, 427-442.
19. Richardson A., 2004: *A probable Roman road and possible Roman bridge at Haresceugh,* Trans. C&WAAS, 3rd Series, IV, 252-257.
20. Richardson A., 2004: *The Romans in the Manchester Area: How they Shaped the Landscape,* published by the author.
21. Richardson A., 2005: *Theoretical Aspects of Roman Camp and Fort Design,* British Archaeological Reports, International Series 1321, Oxford.
22. Richardson A., 2005: *The orientations of Roman camps and forts,* Oxford Journal of Archaeology, Vol. 24, No 4, 415-426.
23. Richardson A., 2006: *The Roman invasion of Cumbria:* Evidence from marching camps, Yearbook of the Matterdale Historical & Archaeological Society, Vol. 13, 8-14. (ISSN 1367 - 6857).

PREFACE

The title of this book makes an assertion that some people will regard as rather bold, but in the following pages I will set out evidence that ought to persuade all but the most sceptical of its credibility. This evidence, most of which has been published in peer-reviewed journals, will be set out in a way that hopefully will make the story more interesting to the general Cumbrian reader curious about the area's past. Those wishing to examine the details should refer to The Roman Survey of Britain, by Michael J. Ferrar and me, as well as my previous papers listed in the Bibliography.

I will treat the subject as the solving of a jig-saw puzzle so that the reader might share in my thirty-odd years of detective work. In this little adventure I enjoyed the co-operation and friendship of three men; Mr George Richardson of Wetheral, Dr Martin Allan of Aberdeen and Mr Richard Bellhouse who has contributed much to our understanding of the Roman Cumberland coastal defences. He had lived at Thursby but had moved to the Midlands when I first met him. I later met and collaborated with Mr Michael Ferrar of Coventry, and his crucial discoveries will be related at the appropriate place.

I arrived in Cumberland in the summer of 1967 and was employed as a veterinary investigation officer at Merrythought, the state veterinary laboratory at Calthwaite. Upon a wall in the main building was a map of Cumbria upon which, in my lunch breaks, I began to mark out the Roman sites and main roads with pins and coloured wool. This was purely a hobby; I had enough interesting professional work which naturally occupied most of my attention. The first thing that struck me was the curiously geometrical lay-out of the road network of minor lanes in the northern half of the county. To give just one example; the Roman road south-westwards from Carlisle seemed to make a right-angle with that approaching the city from the south. Why should this be? The more I looked at the Roman road network, as given in the books, the more unsatisfactory it seemed to be. There were obvious gaps and at the same time there were numerous tantalising clues of a very geometric arrangement of minor roads and lanes; with right-angled bends and discontinuous alignments all over the place. When not trying to solve the mysteries of salmonella infections, which were then ravaging the county's cattle, I thought upon these things and began the quest that I describe in the following pages. Sketch maps are inserted where appropriate but the reader is advised to have the relevant Ordnance Survey maps to hand.

Finally, my justification for the book lies in my wish not to waste the information I have gathered and to stimulate further work. I am especially indebted Michael Ferrar for permission to quote freely from our book and to reproduce some of his diagrams. From him I have learned much that appears in these pages without detailed acknowledgement.

Alan Richardson

16, Thorpefield, Sockbridge, Penrith, Cumbria, CA110 2JN.

December 2007

PART ONE

THE ROMANS IN EAST CUMBERLAND

The Roman army presence

The general outline of the first Roman impact upon Cumbria is well known, though the details are not clear. The most recent authorative exposition is given by Professor David Shotter[1]. The first Roman forces must have arrived in the late 60s AD to establish control over the area but their deployment was part of a greater plan aimed at conquering the whole island. The Tyne-Solway line was marked with a road (*Stanegate*) along a temporarily fortified frontier from which, after a short pause, the Roman forces continued their northwards advance. Between about AD 75 and 90 they were occupied in Scotland but a demand for troops in other parts of the empire led to the garrison being reduced. This resulted in insufficient numbers to hold all the territory between the southern Pennines and the Grampians so the army fell back to the Tyne-Solway line along which eventually Hadrian built his great wall (circa AD 120). This Hadrianic frontier included advanced posts north of the Wall, reserve stations to the south and the fortification of the Cumberland coast as far south as St Bee's Head.

Demand for timber and agricultural produce

The size and organisational complexity of this frontier necessarily required supply depots and an infra-structure of roads and river navigation. The garrison required grain and other foods as well as timber, animals and animal products in enormous quantities. In a paper of 1975, Dr Manning of Cardiff University, argued convincingly that transport costs obliged all Roman army units to obtain as much sustenance as possible locally.[2] He quoted a German study to the effect that a legion needed a support area (*territorium*) of 8,645 acres.[3] This was almost certainly an under-estimate since it gave a "stocking rate", to use a farming term, of about 1.4 men per acre, without considering the needs of draught and cavalry animals and non-combatants. He also estimated that 700 acres were needed to grow the corn for 480 men, without their demand for timber and animal products such as sinew, hides and wool. There was, therefore, every reason for the Romans to exploit the hinterland of the Wall to its maximum. It was immaterial whether the land was good, bad, or indifferent - it had to produce what was needed and reduce the amount to be brought in by ship, wagon and pack animal.

In Hadrian's time, the Wall forts from Birdoswald to Bowness housed units with a nominal strength of 3,808 infantry and 1,408 cavalry.[4] Assuming half as many remounts (reserve animals) were needed, the western Wall alone would account for some 2,000 horses. Maintained on rough pasture close to the forts in summer at one per two acres, they would need 4,000 acres. When not at grass in the winter, or on standby for action, or in training, they would need about five kgs. hay and four kgs. grain per head daily. For 250 days per year, they would need about 2,600 metric tons of each, and assuming a hay yield of one metric ton per acre, a similar number of acres were needed. It has been

---

[1] Shotter (2004)

[2] Manning (1975)

[3] Petrokovits (1960)

[4] Breeze & Dobson (2000)

estimated that a chariot horse needed the annual barley produce of five acres, so another 10,000 acres should be added.[5] A round figure of 17,000 acres might not be far off the mark. To this must be added the corn required by the men, which on Manning's figures, was a further 5,553 acres, giving a total of 22,153 acres. This does not take account of the needs of draught, breeding and growing animals, non-combatants and civilians, nor of the central Wall and coastal forts, nor of those at Old Penrith, Old Carlisle, Brougham and Kirkby Thore. It is probably no exaggeration to say that the Cumberland Wall forts alone needed food for man and beast from at least 35,000 acres. This is equivalent to the combined 19th century arable and pasture acreages of Dalston (10,500), Hesket (15,000) and Skelton (11,000)[6]. This demand, superimposed on the natives' needs, explains why the Roman authorities could not afford to be choosey about the quality of land near the Wall. It is likely that every available acre was pressed into use with customary Roman vigour.

Recognised Roman roads behind Hadrian's Wall

This requirement almost certainly explains why a proportion of the frontier garrison was stationed in forts behind the Wall. But these forces would have needed rapid access to the Wall, as well as an ability to move laterally across its hinterland. However, until the 1980s, the map of the Roman road network in Cumbria north of the Lakes revealed little evidence of any such communication. The generally accepted network related to the Wall comprised the following roads[7].

1. A lateral road immediately behind the Wall and down the Solway coast.
2. Kirkbride-Corbridge, via Carlisle (Stanegate).
3. Carlisle-Papcastle, via Old Carlisle.
4. Old Carlisle-Kirkbride.
5. Carlisle-Brougham, via Old Penrith.
6. Kirkby Thore-Carvoran, via Whitley Castle (Maiden Way)
7. Brougham-Ambleside, (High Street, but with no obvious continuation beyond the High Street Fell summit).
8. Old Penrith-Keswick, via Troutbeck.
9. Keswick, through the Whinlatter Pass to Papcastle and on to Maryport.
10. Maryport to the Papcastle-Carlisle road, north of Mealsgate.

Given the fort distribution in the frontier zone and the need for their rapid mutual support and response, this picture seemed incomplete. There were no links across the central area of the Inglewood and none east of the river Eden. Moreover, we were asked to believe that High Street, crossing the fells above Ullswater, undoubtedly impassable for weeks in winter, was the only connection between Brougham and Ambleside. But any suggestion that this fragmentary network might be improved upon by further research was firmly rejected by academia and the reporting of any new evidence of unrecognised road lines was sternly suppressed.

---

[5] Piggot (1992)

[6] Humphries (1993, 640)

[7] Margaray (1954

Newly recognised Roman roads

Nevertheless, there were plenty of clues both on the map and in the published literature pointing to unrecognised Roman roads in Cumberland. Of course, finding evidence suggestive of a Roman road is not the same as *proving* such a road existed for the grounds for evaluating the evidence are notoriously subjective. Some sceptics will never be convinced without milestones being unearthed in-situ. Nevertheless, the following features are generally accepted as significant and when several occur along a putative road line, their significance greatly increases.

1. *Street and gate* place-names: The first term is derived from Anglo-Saxon and the second from Old Norse; both refer to paved roads. There are so many *gates* in Cumbria that, of itself, the name is probably insignificant. The word, *forth*, which is the same as the modern Welsh, *fford*, also means a road; i.e., Gosforth
2. Mediaeval references to a highway, often a "great" highway (*magna via*), or the king's road (*via regia*): It is generally accepted, though impossible to prove, that roads on straight alignments over several miles were not made between the Roman period and the 18th century. The great R. G. Collingwood regarded these clues as very persuasive.[8]
3. The lines of manor, parish and mediaeval property boundaries, especially when straight for over half a mile.
4. Roman sites or finds of Roman artefacts along the putative road's course.
5. The survival of the causeway: *aggers* (raised banks upon which the causeway sits), together with kerbs, metalling and marginal ditches are typical of Roman engineering but were often copied by later road makers. In some places the Roman aggers were very substantial and though now greatly weathered, they may still stand four to five feet above the surrounding ground.

A somewhat nebulous clue, but one not to be dismissed outright, concerns the place-name element harbour, usually associated with cold, or windy. The term harbour was not originally associated with the sea, but with its broader meaning of keeping and protecting. It is derived from two Anglo-Saxon elements, here, an army, and beorg, a shelter, or refuge.[9] The Anglo-Saxon Chronicle uses the term, here, in a derogatory sense to mean the enemy.[10] Indeed, the word harry indicates what invaders usually did; rob and pillage. Windy and cold harbours were therefore sites, probably fortified, occupied by the enemies of the Anglo-Saxons; that is Danes and Normans. The word cold probably indicated they were old and deserted, even in the middle ages, and windy probably referred to an exposed position. A statistical study has shown that Coldharbours are significantly associated with Roman roads,[11] very probably because these "harriers" used them, but such sites might overlie Roman fortifications. At the very least, harbour place-names are probably evidence of roads in existence at the time of the Scandinavian and Norman invasions.

Over time Roman roads may be repaired and resurfaced with the original line remaining intact, like much of the Penrith-Carlisle (A6) road. But in some places, they disappear; grubbed out and ploughed over. For much of its way, the Roman causeway of the A6 north of Penrith lay about 20 metres west of

---

[8] Collingwood (1937)

[9] Chambers' 20th Century Dictionary (1950)

[10] Brook (1962, 4)

[11] Ogden (1966)

the modern road. Until the 1970's it was visible at Aikbank Common, Calthwaite (OS 348.70 541.25).[12] The *agger* is still visible where it climbs a steep bank north of Bulls Head Farm (OS 348.95 540.00). Often, Roman road sections were worn away, mended and re-mended with line shifting over the years. Often, new lengths replaced old ones with the course of the route shifting quite significantly. Any given Roman road is likely to show all of these signs of evolution and may have become quite unrecognisable. There are, without doubt, many roads still in use that were originally laid down by Roman engineers but whose carriageways no longer precisely follow their original lines and which, over the ages, have lost all clues to their origin. As rights of way, they may be regarded as the "legal descendants" of Roman roads; much as Grandfather's axe, with three new handles and two new heads, remains Grandfather's axe.

By collecting these sorts of clues from the map, from the published literature and from inspecting the ground and by excavating suspect causeways, the combined efforts of George Richardson, Martin Allan and myself eventually led to the recognition of more Roman roads. They have been described in published reports and are listed thus:

1. Troutbeck-Ambleside, via Matterdale and the Kirkstone Pass.[13]
2. *Appleby Street*, along the foot of the Eastern Fells from Castrigg on the A66 near Appleby, via Long Marton, Milburn, Ousby, Melmerby, Gamblesby, Renwick and Castle Carrock. It probably connected with Castlesteads on the Wall.[14] [15]
3. Brougham-Troutbeck, across the northern Lake District and to the west coast via Keswick and the Whinlatter Pass.[16]

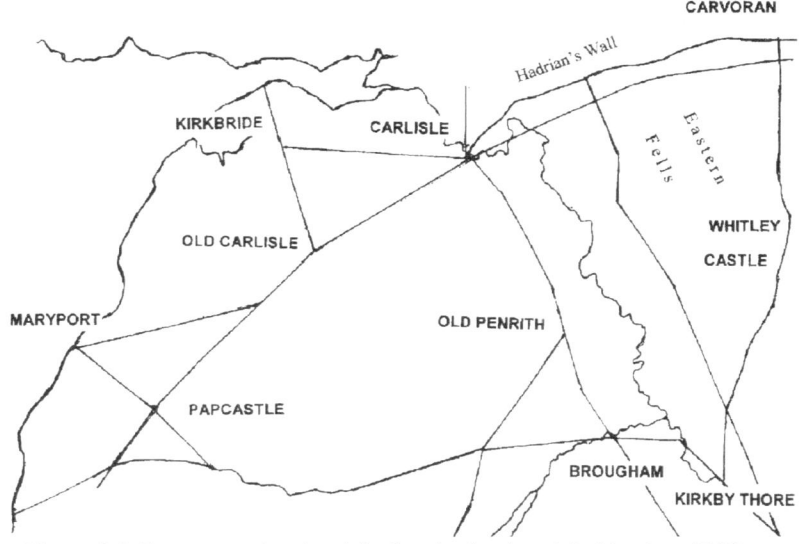

Figure 1.1: Roman road network in Cumberland updated to circa 1990

Following these findings the Roman road network in eastern Cumbria could now be amended to that shown in Figure 1.1.

---

[12] The late Mr M. Savage of Aikbank, Calthwaite, removed much of it in the 1970s
[13] Richardson & Allan (1990)
[14] Richardson (1984)
[15] Richardson (2002)
[16] Allan (1994)

Remaining evidence of unrecognised Roman roads

Nevertheless, this updated picture remained incomplete for there were still plenty of clues pointing to other roads, particularly several street place-names marked on the OS map or recorded in the literature. These are listed in Table 1.1 on the next page, but four of them merit further description.

Itonfield Street*

Itonfield Street, between Braithwate and Ivegill School, was probably the Roman road crossing Broadfield mentioned by Messrs Lysons in 1816. Located in the former Inglewood Forest, it was marked on Hodkinson and Donald's (1770s) map as a short

TABLE 1.1 "STREET" PLACE-NAMES IN EAST CUMBRIA NOT ASSOCIATED WITH KNOWN ROMAN ROADS

Place	Parish	OS grid or literary reference
OS map		
Street House	Ainstable	354.10 547.20
Itonfield Street	Hesket	Through 342.00 544.10
Street Head Farm	Hesket	342.90 542.42
Street Field	Hesket	343.00 542.30
The Street and Street Head	Hesket Newmarket	333.50 530.50
How Street	Hayton	Along northing 557.00
Street House	Hayton	350.00 557.00
Literature		
Thief Street	Hayton	Graham (1907): 1866 OS map
Brampton Street	Carlattan	Graham (1920)
The Street	Armathwaite and Castle Carrock	Anon (undated)
Hee Street	Cotehill, Wetheral	Prescott (1877) Bowey (1715)
Near & Far Street Close (1817)	Hesket	Armstrong *et al* (undated, 206)
Low Street (1597)	Hesket	ditto
Lytle Street (1722)	Hesket	ditto
Plumpton Street	Plumpton	Hodkinson & Donald (1770-75)
Street Dale & Street Field	Castle Carrock	Armstrong *et al* (undated, 75)
Street Field, Saughtreegate	Heads Nook	Richardson (1984)

straight section running roughly north-westwards from *Street Head Farm*, Low Braithwaite, before bending westwards to Ivegill village. The straight section is now modern road and it lies on the same perfectly straight alignment as five other widely separate sections of road. They are, Hutton Row, Morton Mill Road (Calthwaite), a short road section at Low Grange (Low Braithwaite), the road through Unthank and Green Lane, Pow Bank, Dalston. The line's inclination is about NNW - SSE and it is about nine miles long. See Figure 1.2. It seems that these modern roads, laid out at the enclosure of 1819, were set upon a pre-existing line. On Hodkinson and Donald's map, its

---

**Hodkinson and Donald's map (circa 1770) shows Itonfield Street bending away towards Ivegill. I shall restrict the name to the straight section between Street Head Farm, Low Braithwaite, and Ivegill School.

[17] Lyson & Lyson (1816, 147)

southern part is marked by a track over unenclosed ground between Hutton Row and Thomas Close and three clues suggest this track was perfectly straight.

1. A crop mark in a pasture at the northern end of Morton Mill Road (OS 344.45 540.10) consisting of a wide, dry, strip, margined by rushes, was photographed by me in 1980 before the field was disturbed by tree planting and the feature lost. See Plates 1 and 2. The crop mark was over 20 feet wide and consistent with the base of an *agger* that has been levelled.
2. The course of the *Lyne* Beck, which continues the line north of the crop mark towards Street Head Farm, Low Braithwaite, is straddled by many large stones, not otherwise abundant in the locality, suggesting disturbed kerbs and metalling.
3. The name of the Lyne Beck, forming the parish boundary, may be derived from *limes*, as in Cheshire where it is often associated with boundary roads.[18]

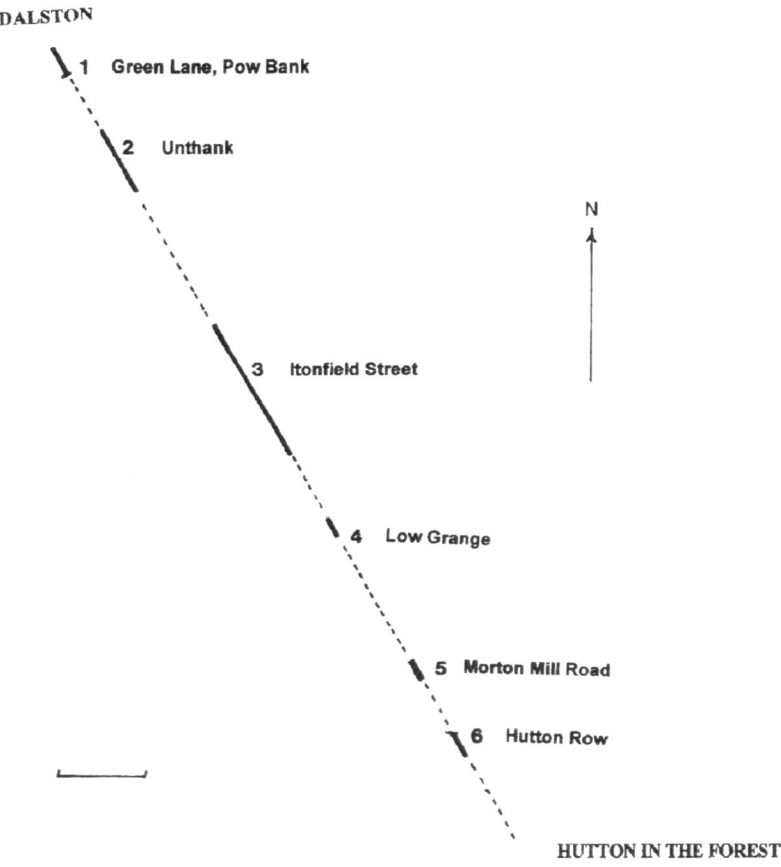

Figure 1.2: Alignment of certain lanes between Dalston and Hutton-in-the-Forest. (Scale mark = 1 km)

The Inglewood Forest boundary

The Inglewood forest, created after the Norman Conquest, covered a large area west of the Eden between Penrith and Carlisle. In 1301, its western boundary went from Carlisle along the Roman road towards Papcastle as far as the river Wampool, near Wigton. It then followed several water courses, "to the head of Rowland beck; and from that place

---

[18] Dodgson (1970, 4)

descending to the waters of Caldbeck; and so down by that water to the place where Caldbeck falls into Caldew. And so up to Gyrgwath; and so by the highway of Sourby unto Stanewath under the castle of Sourby; and so by the highway up to Mabil cross; and so to the hill of Kenwathen, going down by the said highway through the middle of the town of Alleynby (Ellonby); and so by the same way through the middle of the town of Blencowe; and so by the same way unto Pelat (Pallet Hill); and so going down by the same way unto the bridge of Amote (Eamont); and so from that bridge going down by the bank Amote (Eamont) unto Eden."[19]

These references to hard stone ways clearly refer to roads of some sort. The hard stone way of Sowerby is almost certainly the stretch of road between Hesket Newmarket and Millhouse, now known as *Salter Lonning*. This *salter* name is certainly mediaeval and refers to the main commodity transported along such routes.[20] Though not bound to follow Roman roads, many saltways certainly did. At Hesket Newmarket, Salter Lonning joins the *Street*, passing just south of Caldbeck as far as Park End.

A forest boundary change in the reign of Henry II mentioned a road from Pallet Hill near Penrith (OS 547.50 530.50) to Uldale, via Haltcliffe and Caldbeck and then by "the old King's road" to the river Ellen.[21] It looks as though the *Street* between Hesket Newmarket and Park End was this "old King's road". Southwest of Park End, an *agger* can be traced over the unenclosed Ellerbeck Common for about half a mile from Greenrigg (OS 329.30 538.55) to a field at OS 328.20 538.20. Very curiously, within this field, the *agger* is much more substantial than upon the open moor, as if the enclosure preserved it from attrition, but when traced through the neighbouring enclosures it fades out again. In short, there is sound evidence of a mediaeval and probably Roman route from Eamont Bridge to the river Ellen near Uldale, via Blencowe, Ellonby, Mabil Cross, Sowerby and Caldbeck.

A possible pre-Roman road between Carlisle and Penrith

In the late 19th century, a "pre Roman" road from Carlisle to Penrith, running west of the A6 (Roman road) was suggested by Chancellor Ferguson, a man with an immense knowledge of Cumbrian antiquities.[22] He based his hypothesis on place-names and local tradition and postulated that it went from Etterby Wath on the Eden west of the city, "up Willow Holme" by existing lanes to Upperby and thence to Wreay, and so by way of Low Street, Plumpton, to Penrith; thus running a short distance west of the main Brougham-Carlisle Roman road (A6). Ferguson clearly felt that two parallel Roman roads so close together was inconceivable and concluded that this route must have been pre-Roman.

Via Regia and Hee Street

In 1976, the late Mr Paul Wilson drew attention to several mediaeval references to roads between Penrith and Carlisle going east of the A6 road and west of the river Eden. They included a pack-horse road at Aiketgate, the *Hee Street* south of Cotehill, towards Black Moss Pool, and the *via regia* at Lazonby. He suggested these were remnants of another ancient route that seemed to duplicate needlessly the Brougham-Carlisle Roman road A6.[23]

---

[19] Mannix & Whellan (1847)
[20] Crump (1939)
[21] Forest Proceedings (1217), Chancery, 17. cited in Mannix and Whelan (1847).
[22] Ferguson (1886)
[23] Wilson (1976)

Discussion

If all these clues really pointed to Roman roads, as in most contexts they certainly would, their distribution was truly baffling. See Figure 1.3. A route from the river Eamont near Penrith towards Caldbeck might represent a lost connection between the fort at Brougham and Old Carlisle, Wigton, and the Solway coast. But Chancellor Ferguson's Etterby - Penrith road running west of the A6 and Wilson's similarly postulated route east of that road could not be plausibly reconciled with the authentic Roman road (A6). Perhaps the scattered references were to local roads of the type the Romans called *viae vicanae*, made for transporting produce from farms to the main roads and river navigation points. Throughout Britain there must have been hundreds of such roads whose provenance has been lost. Perhaps there was no planned network at all, and these scattered clues were merely the echoes of a hotch-potch of lanes that had served the area from time immemorial.

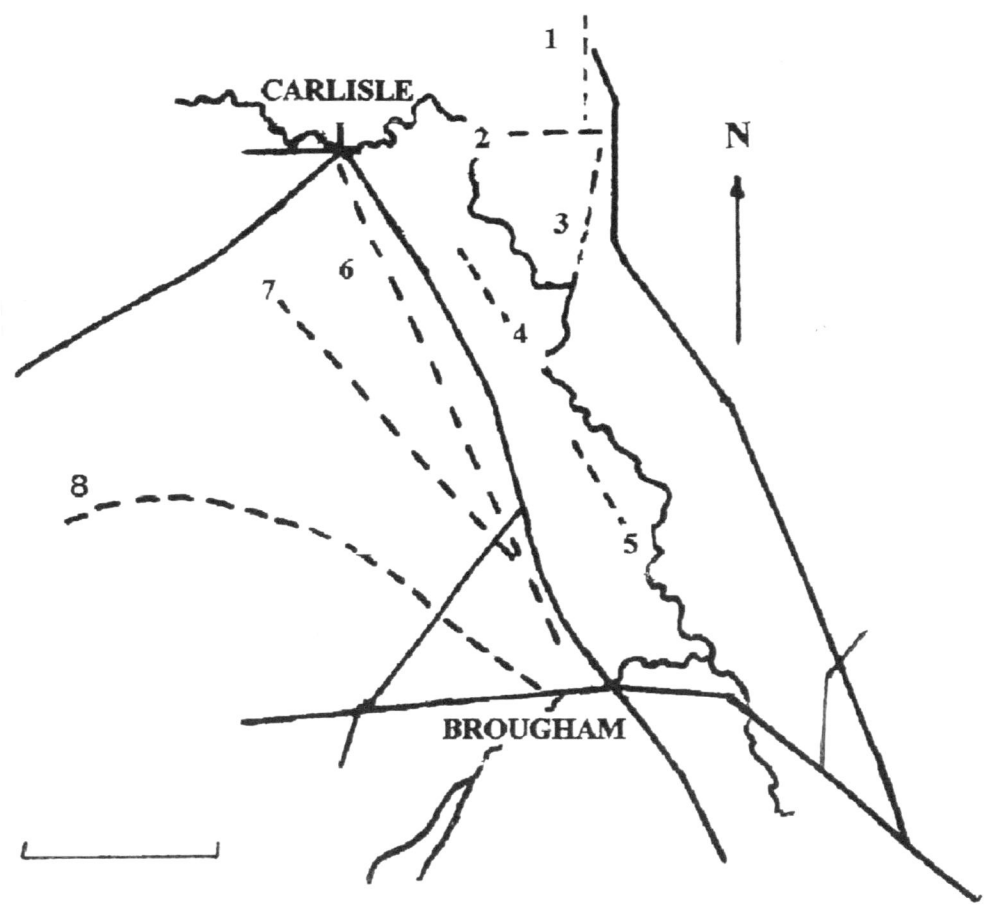

Figure 1.3: Clues to some ancient roads between Carlisle and Penrith: Authentic Roman roads shown as bold lines. Scale = 7 miles. (1) Thief Street: (2) How Street: (3) The Street or Brampton Street: (4) Hee Street: (5) via regia: (6) Ferguson's Pre Roman road: (7) Itonfield Street line: (8) Inglewood Forest boundary road.

Then, in 1971, a new book threw an interesting new light on the whole problem.

***

Plate 1: Behind the pylon in the mid ground is a crop mark of *limes* D6W of cadaster B at Morton Mill Road, Calthwaite (OS 344.45 540.10).

Plate 2: The same feature at ground level. The site has since been planted with trees.

PART TWO

A ROMAN SURVEY IN EAST CUMBERLAND

The Corpus Agrimensorum Romanorum

In 1971, Oswald Dilke, Professor of Latin at the University of Leeds, published *The Roman Land Surveyors: An Introduction to the Agrimensores*.[1] In this book he summarised the salient points from a body of Roman texts known as the *Corpus Agrimensorum Romanorum* that lay scattered throughout several great libraries. This work has now been greatly supplemented by Dr. Brian Campbell of Queen's University, Belfast.[2] The *corpus* comprises documents by several Roman authors which presumably survived through the Middle Ages because they were useful to the monasteries and other landed interests. They record how the Romans surveyed land, made maps, or *formae*, and distributed plots to the citizenry. The work was carried out by professional surveyors, or *agrimensores*, who had the duty of submitting plans and land ownership details to the authorities. The main features of the system, which was known as *centuriation*, were as follows:

1. Using a primitive, but accurate, sort of theodolite (*groma*), land was divided into *centuriae* which were rectangular, normally square, plots by a matrix of boundaries, or *limites* (singular, *limes*) crossing at right angles. The word *limes* is derived from the Latin for *mud*, because they were often muddy tracks, as opposed to metalled roads. In some places, the *limites* might be ditches or mere baulks of earth. In others they were well-made roads.

2. The *groma* was a staff upon which were mounted two cross arms set at right angles and from whose ends plumb bobs were suspended. See Figure 2.1. It was set up vertically and after sighting, the lines werepegged out across country. When done carefully, this was very accurate.

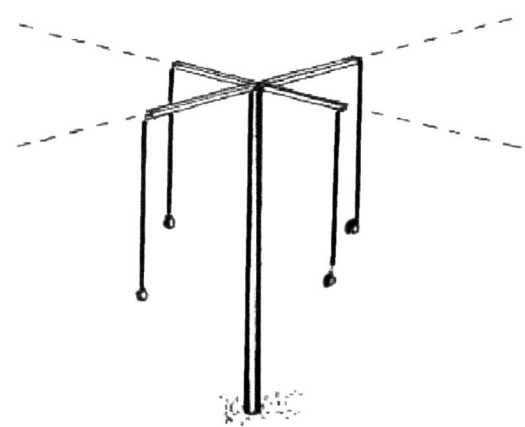

Figure 2.1: The *groma*

3. The starting point of the survey was the *tetrans*, a point from which two main axes were set out at right angles; the *kardo maximus* (KM) and the *decumanus maximus* (DM). The parallel *limites* were known as *kardines* and *decumani* respectively.

---

[1] Dilke (1971)
[2] Campbell (1996)

4. The orientation of the grid varied. Typically the *kardo* was on the latitude and the *decumanus* on the meridian, the directions being determined by sun-dial. But often the grid was off-set to suit the land relief and its natural drainage.
4. The unit of length was the *actus* of 120 Roman feet (one Roman foot = 11.65 inches). The area measure was an *actus quadratus* (120 x 120 Roman feet.).
5. Typically, but not invariably, the *centuriae* were 20 *actus* (2,400 Roman feet) square, but there were non-standard squares and rectangles. They were identified with a reference code inscribed on wooden, or stone, posts (*cippi*). I shall often use the term *centuria* to mean a distance of 20 *actus* (2,400 Roman feet) though strictly speaking it is an area measure.
6. Each *centuria* was further divided into plots by a regular network of baulks or ditches.
7. Every fifth *limes* (100 a*ctus*) in each direction was set out with special care and squared off with the *groma* to prevent the accumulation of errors. These were known as *quintariae* and, by law of Augustus, were roads 20 feet wide.[3]
8. The government first allocated these plots, but thereafter they could be bought and sold.

Centuriation was not associated with any particular farming system; the land could comprise arable, pasture and woodland.[4] Its purpose was to establish boundaries, to define property rights, tax liability and avoid disputes. With new colonies, drawing lots for the plots assured fair shares to the settlers.[5] Despite these safeguards, some allocations of poor land to army veterans provoked protests.[6] Not all newly-centuriated land was necessarily taken up and the unallocated portions, even within the *centuriae*, could be put to communal use or, in the case of conquered territory, returned to its former owners.[7]

The land therefore had imposed upon it a grid of boundaries and from the air would have looked like a chessboard of large fields divided into smaller plots. The boundaries within the *centuriae* were ditches or paths giving access to the plots. The landholders knew exactly which plots they held and, most importantly, so did the government. A surveyed area, duly marked out and recorded, was called a *cadaster* and the record was used for tax assessment. At Orange, in the Rhone valley, the *cadaster* was recorded upon tiles set up in a fine, public portico within the Roman city, and this was probably done elsewhere.[8]

The method of centuriation was derived from Greek and Etruscan practice but the Romans brought it to a fine art, eventually centuriating huge areas in Mediterranean countries. Scholars have described cadasters in Italy, Tunisia, Greece and southern Gaul. [9] [10] [11] The most northerly was at Orange, though Dilke identified possible examples in Kent and Sussex[12] and I have described two, and possibly three, at Manchester. [13] The *agrimensores*

---

[3] Chevallier (1976, 66)
[4] Campbell 1996, 80)
[5] Campbell 1996, 92)
[6] Campbell (1996, 96)
[7] Campbell (1996, 91)
[8] Dilke (1971)
[9] Dilke (1971)
[10] Bradford (1957)
[11] Hardie (1965)
[12] I have set out the evidence of at least two, and possibly three, cadasters at Manchester (Richardson 2004 a)

were numerate and literate men who understood mathematics and geometry, and their whole practice was closely associated with religion and augury. The boundaries, once legally set out, were literally sacrosanct and meddling with them was a sacrilegious crime. See Figure 2.2.

Cadasters in Cumbria

Here was a possible explanation for the confusing distribution of clues to Roman roads in our district. Was it possible that Itonfield Street and the other lanes on the nine-mile line from Dalston to Hutton Row were remnants of a *limes* rather than a main road? A closer look at the map then revealed another line of discontinuous lanes running at right angles to the nine-mile line, between Middlesceugh Hall and Barrow Mill on the river Petteril and crossing it at Street Head Farm, Low Braithwaite. The distance from Itonfield Street to Barrow Mill was equal to four *centuriae* (4 x 2,400 Roman feet, or 80 actus) and the distance from Itonfield Street to the Skelton-Middlesceugh road, to which it ran parallel, was the same. In between these two, at an interval of 40 *actus* was another shorter, parallel road from Unthank to Scales Hall. This looked promising.

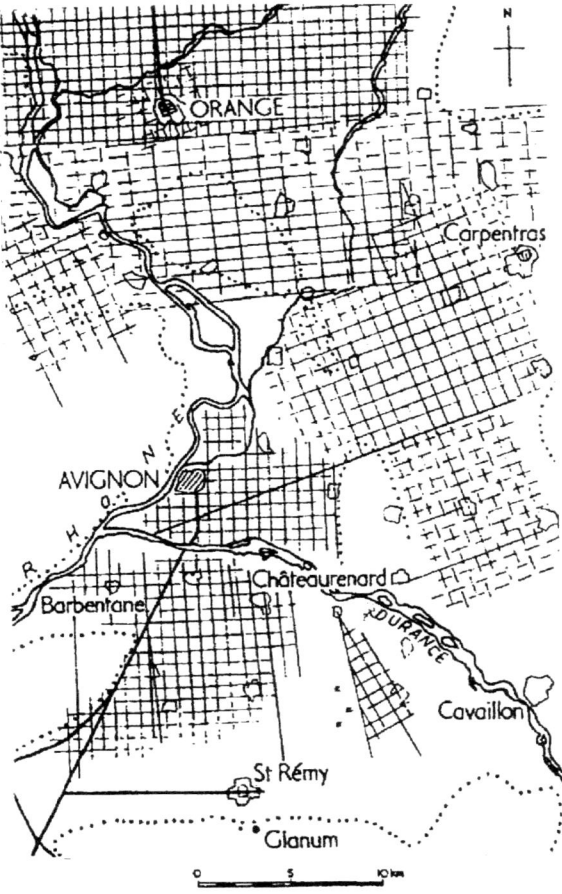

Figure 2.2: Cadasters in the Rhone valley (After Dilke 1971 by kind permission of Mrs M Dilke)

When a sheet of tracing paper ruled with a 20 *actus* scale grid was placed over the map so that one line overlay Itonfield Street, a large number of other roads and boundaries throughout Hesket and Calthwaite, and even further afield, was found to coincide with the grid lines; including the *Hee Street*, south of Cotehill. The area of exploration was widened and it became clear that the Middlesceugh Hall-Barrow Mill line was 400 *actus* (20 *centuriae*,

---

[13] Richardson (2004)

or five *quintariae*) from the point where Hadrian's Wall crossed the R. Eden at Carlisle. A line parallel to the Barrow Mill-Middlesceugh Hall axis was tangential to the curve of the Wall at that point. See Figure 2.3. Moreover, when the Middlesceugh-Barrow Mill line was projected eastwards, it coincided with a short length of lane at High Northsceugh (OS 353.00 548.10) some 20 *centuriae* east of the Itonfield Street line. The place-names suggest that at some remote date, this *limes* defined the north and middle parts of a wood (*sceugh*). Even more curious was the fact that at 20 *centuriae* from Middlesceugh along the same line to the WSW, where one might have expected a "south sceugh," was a farmstead known as Hutton Sceugh, (OS 353.15 537.70)

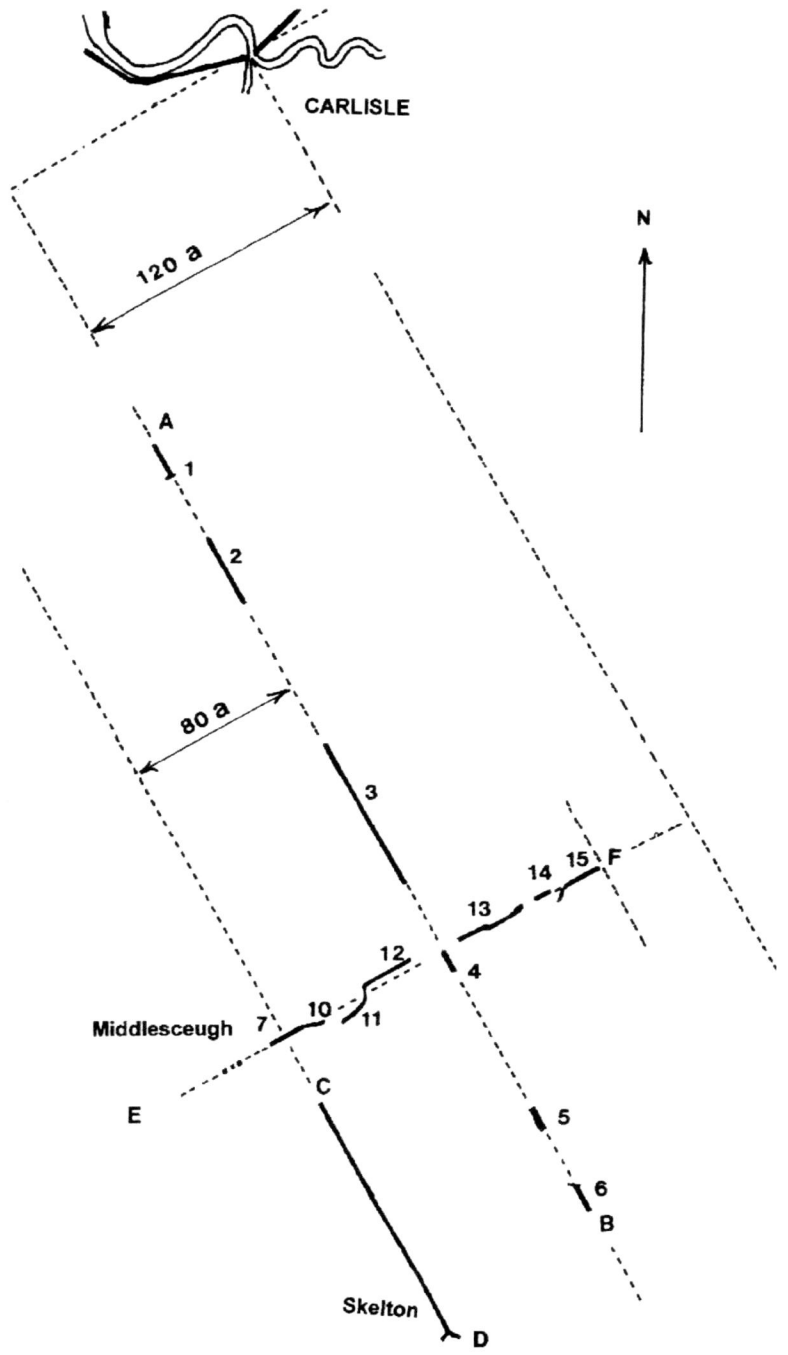

Figure 2.3: Remnants of *limites* south of Carlisle (scale a = one *actus*)

It was also clear that the roughly NNW inclination of the nine-mile Itonfield Street line ran parallel to the main Brougham - Carlisle Roman road (A6) between High Hesket and Scalesceugh. This road section was itself apparently aligned on the section of Roman road between Reagill and Brougham, known as the *Street*, over 12 miles to the south.[14] Thus, a geometric relationship, in terms of an orthogonal (square) grid, was established between Hadrian's Wall, the Itonfield Street line, Hee Street and the Street south of Brougham. The relevant area was about 30 x 10 miles. This was very promising. See Figure 2.4.

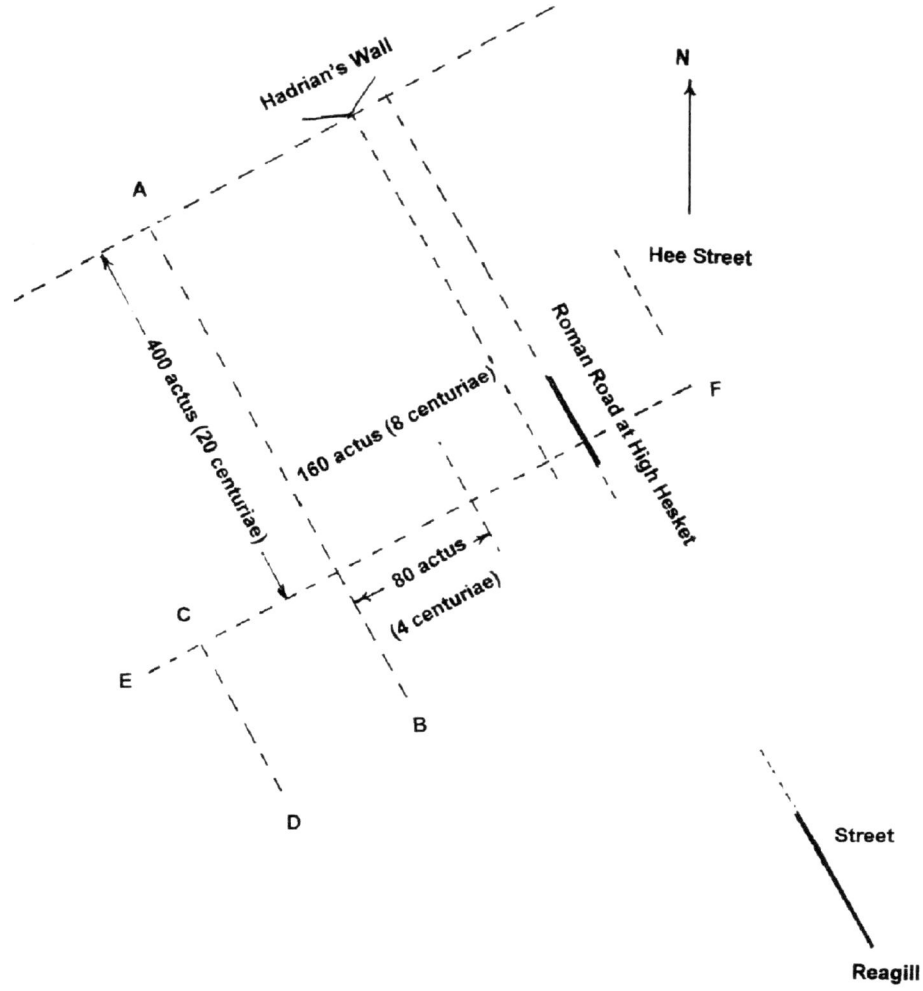

Figure 2.4: Geometric relationship of Roman roads, Hadrian's Wall and limites : (AB = line of Itonfield Street: CD = Middlesceugh Hall-Skelton: EF = Middlesceugh Hall-Barrow Mill)

Interestingly, certain of the main road lines of this now hypothetical cadaster were in existence in the 1770s, when shown on the map of Hodkinson and Donald. This suggested they could well have been the remnants of a matrix of lanes that had lain largely undisturbed in the Inglewood Forest since Roman days, to be incorporated into the local road system at the enclosure. But the enclosure was a piecemeal business. After the Norman Conquest, the Forest was divided into a number of holdings, known as *serjeanties*, and these imply the existence, or creation, of boundaries of some sort.

---

[14] Ross (1920)
[15] Summerson (1991, 60)

As early as the 13th century, Lord Dacre had enclosed land near Middlesceugh at the northern end of the Skelton-Middlesceugh road line.[16] A field at Skelton in 1604 was known as *Mydle Sceuth yate* [17] which could only refer to the Skelton-Middlesceugh road, connecting the 13th century enclosure to that made at Skelton 500 years later Another interesting observation concerned the farm known as Devonshire Square in Hesket parish; the farm buildings stood in the dead centre of a *centuria*, suggesting that the boundaries were evident when the enclosure was made. An outline of the main grid lines between Hutton in the Forest and Carlisle is shown in Figure 2.5.

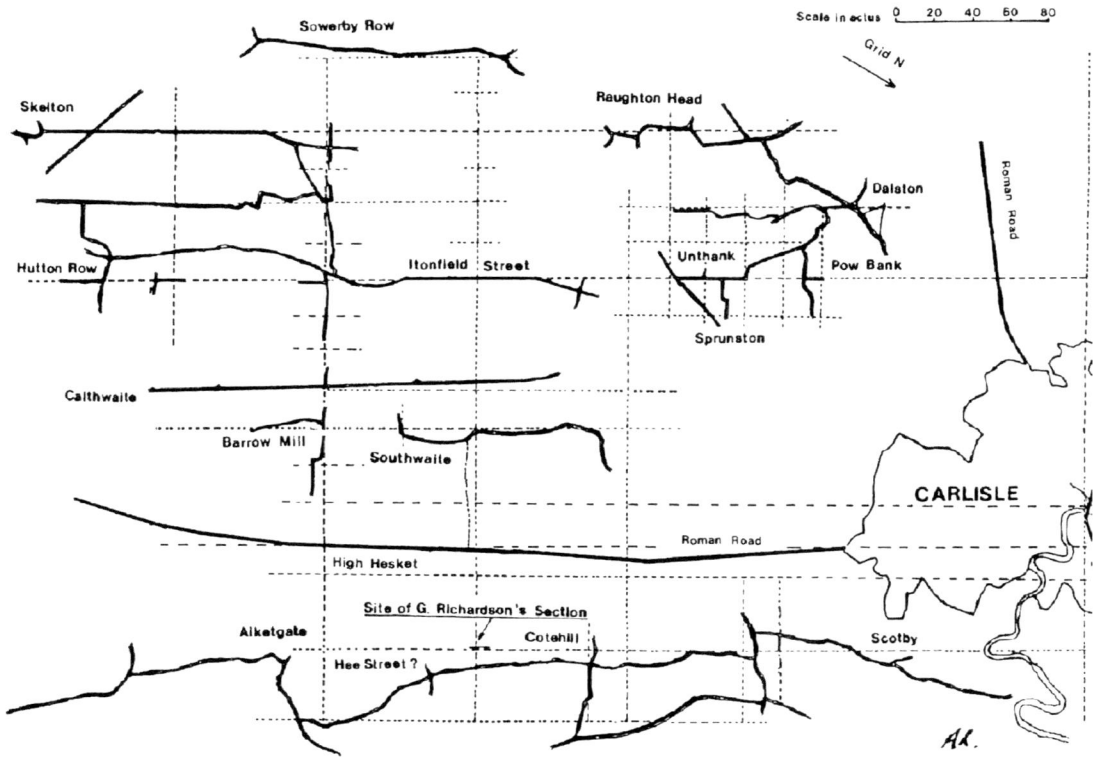

Figure 2.5: Evidence of the cadaster south of Carlisle

The putative cadaster appeared to stretch from the river Eden at Carlisle, being confined by the river Caldew to the west and the river Eden to the east. With very little imagination, it could be seen to extend as far as Askham, south of Penrith, where many lanes and field boundaries tended to fit with the grid. When this grid was drawn on the map, relatively few modern features overlay the actual *limites* but, a vast number of minor lanes and field boundaries were aligned parallel to them. The cadaster appeared to be inclined about 30 W of N.

A similar tracing paper exercise then revealed the probable existence of another cadaster at Hayton, east of Carlisle, which George Richardson had noticed. This was orientated on the cardinal points, with two roads running EW; How Street and the Hayton village main street which were one *centuria* apart, with Fenton Gate (NS) connecting them.

---

[16] Higham (1986, 94)
[17] Armstrong et al, (undated, 206)

Thief Street ran obliquely across the eastern end of this area of this apparently separate cadaster. See Figure 2.6.

When these preliminary evidences of centuriation were duly submitted for publication, they caused "some fluttering in the academic dove cote" and were rejected, but Professor Dilke intervened and the papers duly appeared.[18] [19] I continued to collect further information and from the map of Thomas Bowey who made a sketch of boundaries south of Carlisle about the year 1715, came evidence of other lost *limites* in Hesket parish.[20] Bowey's map shows three long boundary hedges, extant at the end of the 17th century. Although this map is free-hand drawn, their lengths and general direction can be determined from features identifiable on the modern map.

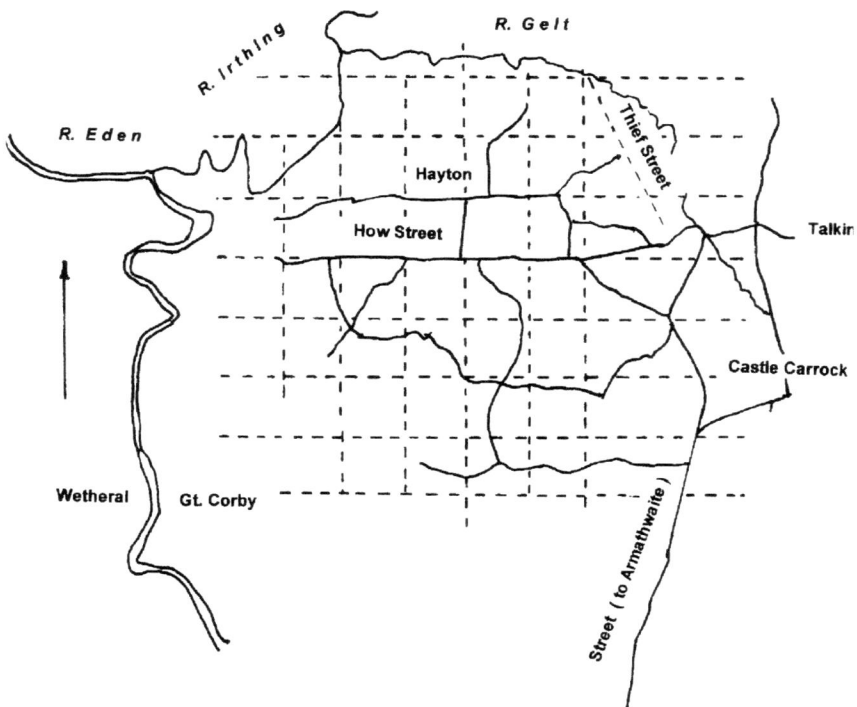

Figure 2.6: Evidence of the cadaster east of Carlisle

One "old hedge" accompanied the *High Street*, that is the *Hee Street*, between Cotehill and Aiketgate, parallel to, and probably co-incident with a *limes* 10 *centuriae* east of the Itonfield Street line. The *Castle Hewen Boundary Hedge* was also parallel to Itonfield Street. It ran for over a mile from Tarn Wadling to the slate quarry north of Barrock Fell, nine *centuriae* east of (and parallel to) the Itonfield Street line. Connecting both at right angles was another "Old Hedge", roughly four *centuriae* north of the Middlesceugh-Barrow Mill line, going from the slate quarry ENE to just north of the *Tackengate Stone*. Moreover, there was yet another, the *Barrock Fold Hedge*, running along the seventh *limes* east of Itonfield Street, from Scalesceugh to Court Thorn, on the Roman Road north of High Hesket,

---

[18] Richardson (1982)

[19] Richardson (1986)

[20] Bowey (1715)

where the feudal lords and tenants of the Inglewood Forest traditionally met to transact Forest business.[21] Court Thorn proves to be one *centuria* north of the Middlesceugh Hall-Barrow Mill line. It is the precise spot where an intersection of *limites* meets the Roman road and there could have been some sort of inscribed monument set up here by the *agrimensores* to invite the curiosity of later ages. There is not a better explanation as to why this particular place should have become a meeting place. Finally, on Bowey's map, the boundary of the Carlisle Dean and Chapter land seems to have followed another *limes* from Wragmire towards the river Eden. A tradition of another "ancient British" track between Tarn Wadling and Aiketgate, i.e., possibly along a *limes* eight *centuriae* east of Itonfield Street, was recorded by a local inhabitant in recent times.[22] These features are shown in Figure 2.7

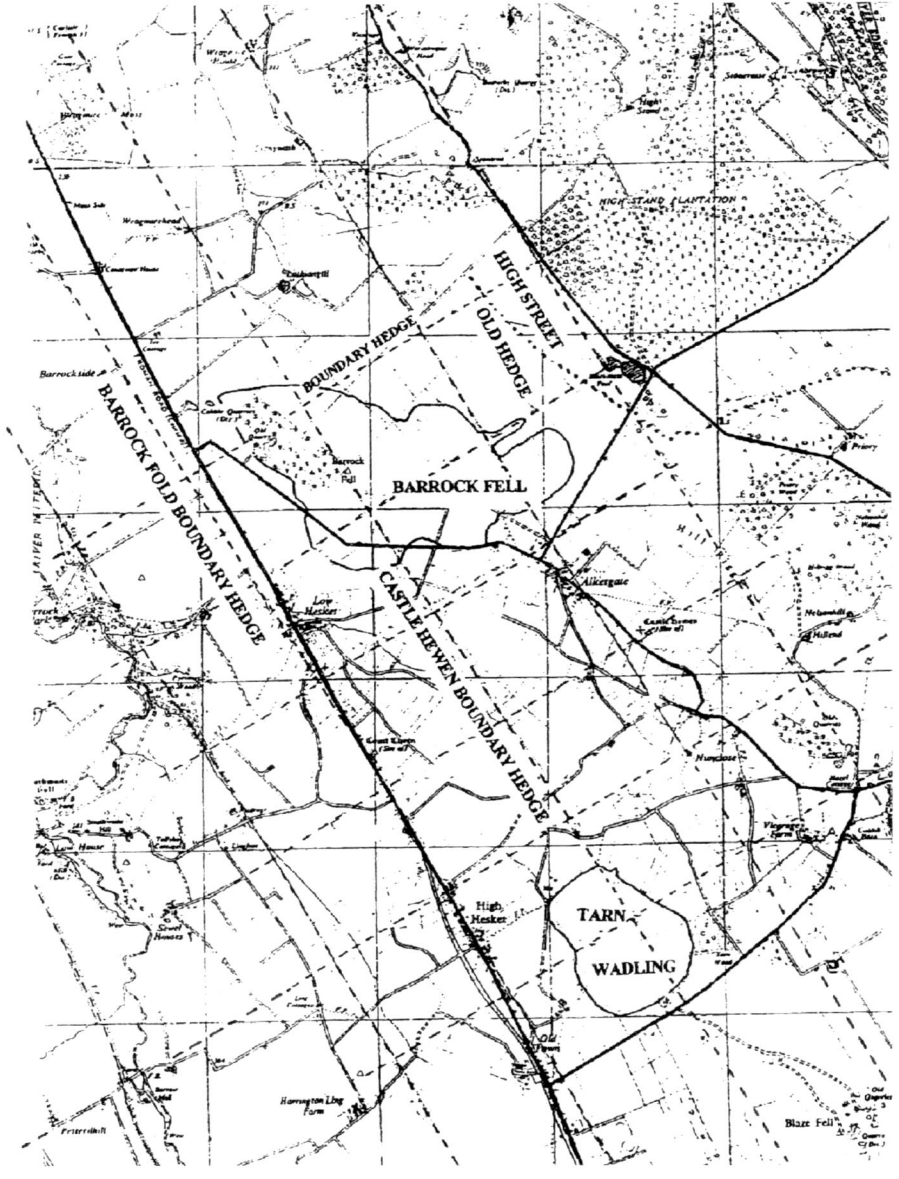

Figure 2.7: Limites persisting as boundary hedges in 1715 (From Bowey's map)

---

[21] Hutchinson (1794-7, 504)

[22] McGillivray (undated)

I was now satisfied there was evidence of two Roman cadasters. George Richardson, a most cautious and conscientious man, agreed. The sceptics did not but I was encouraged by Professor Dilke who told me that his researches into centuriation had not been welcomed by the archaeological establishment. I therefore felt justified in collecting more data and in examining more closely the geometric relationships of the several putative survey lines that had emerged. For convenience I shall now refer to the cadaster whose *limites*, aligned on the cardinal points, are detectable at Hayton as cadaster A. The other cadaster whose *limites* are evident in Hutton and Calthwaite will be cadaster B

I then discovered a place-name clue that had been around for a century. In 1892 Dr Taylor had proposed that the name of Catterlen was derived from the old Irish, meaning the quadrangle (*caether*)[24] at the marsh by the river (*leana*).[23] This must have seemed very odd at the time and later place-name experts ignored it and preferred to believe that the *caether* was derived from old Welsh, meaning chair. I suggest that Taylor was correct and the quadrangle the Irish settlers found was a *centuria*.

Another piece of the jig-saw appeared in 2001 in a paper by Dr A. Breeze, a place-name expert from the University of Salamanca.[25] I had speculated that the name of the river Petteril, which flowed through the putative Inglewood cadaster, might have been derived from the Latin word *pertica*, the *agrimensore's* measuring rod, which has given rise to similar place-names elsewhere, as well as the land measure we know as the *perch*. I had consulted place-name experts without enlightenment; then Dr. Breeze argued very persuasively that it was derived from the old Celtic word, *petryal*, for a rectangle, or square. He did not know of the cadaster in the Inglewood and thought the word was associated with graves. He has since revised his opinion.[26] We can now reasonably suggest that the river owes its name to its flowing through land marked out in squares, though it is generally thought that river names derive from the remotest antiquity, rather than the Roman period.

The alignment of the cadasters

It was evident that cadaster A was aligned on the cardinal points, that is along the latitude and the meridian, a common practice in the Mediterranean countries where a fair share of sun and shade for the occupiers was regarded as important. But when measured by protractor, the Itonfield Street line in cadaster B inclined some $30°$ W of N. Where cadasters were not aligned on the cardinal points their lay-out was often associated with the water courses and interestingly at Florence the cadaster was off-set from the main EW road through the city by $31°$ E of N, virtually the same angle.[27] But what an odd angle! Clearly it was important to the *agrimensores* but unless cadaster B's inclination could be measured accurately; I could not make any meaningful deductions about it nor find the site of the *tetrans*. Determining the angle precisely therefore became the major challenge.

At that time it was generally held that Roman roads were laid out over long distances by surveyors placing beacons on hilltops and the engineers driving the roads towards them.

---

[23] Taylor (1892, 9)
[24] Armstrong et al (undated, vol. xx, 182)
[25] Breeze (2001)
[26] Breeze A (personal communication)
[27] Hardie (1965)

I therefore looked for a similar point that might have been the *tetrans* for the Inglewood cadaster and guessed it may have been on a hill just north of Penrith.[28] But the more I thought about it, the less satisfactory this seemed. Commonly, the *tetrans* was in the forum of a newly planted city, and since cadaster B seemed to tie-in with Hadrian's Wall at the point where it crossed the river Eden, I shifted the search to the Carlisle area. By extending the grid with ruler and pencil across the map, I found a point close to Carlisle cathedral that looked promising. It was 20 *actus* E and 20 *actus* S of the Wall's crossing the river Eden, having allowed for a 30° rotation. But there were limitations to this approach because small angle errors are magnified by distance and drawing long lines accurately on maps requires the professional skill and equipment of a draughtsman. I had access to neither and for a number of years made no further progress.

Defining cadastral grid lines by calculation

When home computers became available I made a spreadsheet to calculate the OS co-ordinates for any point on an orthogonal grid, relative to a fixed datum, the distances being in *actus*. This allowed me to find the exact OS grid reference for the node (intersection) of any two *limites* on a grid tilted at any given angle. The formulae are given in Appendix 1. The spreadsheet was written to give the grid references of four quadrant points at set distances from the datum point. It overcame the errors arising from manipulating a long ruler over two map sheets glued together, but the results depended critically on the angle of inclination. The method also had its limitations over distance, due to the earth's curvature; an OS map, being a flat depiction of a curved surface, is slightly inaccurate at the edges. Thus, it became even more important to define the angle accurately. Later, I devised another spreadsheet to give the co-ordinates of any point, in terms of *actus* and *centuriae*, from a given OS datum point. This is explained in Appendix 2.

So, to make best use of these spreadsheets, I needed to discover the precise inclination of the Itonfield Street line. This was easy using trigonometry. One simply took the grid references for each end-point, i.e., at Green Lane, Pow Bank, and at the south end of Hutton Row, and found the differences in northings (**n**) and eastings (**e**). Because the alignment is the hypotenuse of a right-angled triangle, the *Tangent* of the angle was **e/n**. Taking the grid references from the map with a ruler and set-square at each end of the line and at the ends of each separate section and then pooling the results of the calculation, gave a figure of about 30.5°. But even this relied heavily on reading the map accurately and, given the map scale, there was bound to be some error. I therefore concluded somewhat doubtfully that the Romans had intended it to be 30° W of N, though for what reason, other than the general lie of the land, I could not imagine, unless it was that the angle was one third of a right-angle. With the spreadsheet, I then investigated the effect of altering this by fractions of a degree around 30°, with a view to locating a plausible *tetrans* within Roman Carlisle.

The Roman road between Carlisle and Reagill

As I pondered the problem I began to see that if the survey was as extensive as it seemed to be, the same *tetrans* may also have served as the survey point for the road approaching

---

[28] Richardson (1986)

Carlisle from the south. It will be remembered that the Itonfield Street line appeared to be parallel to this road between High Hesket and Scalesceugh, as well as to the *Street* south of Brougham. But this alignment was not integral to the Inglewood cadaster because its distance from Itonfield Street was not a whole number of *centuriae*, except at Court Thorn. Moreover, on close inspection, the (A6) road alignment turned out to be not strictly parallel to the Itonfield Street line. When determined by trigonometry, between Street House, south of Brougham, and Scalesceugh, it was 25.88° not 30° ; a discrepancy of some 4°. Nor did the road alignment run into Carlisle city, but to Stanwix on the east, a fact first established by Percival Ross (1920). This, consideration, taken together with not knowing for certain whether the selected grid reference points actually overlay the Roman causeway, and considering the magnifying effect of distance on minute angle errors, meant that no absolute reliance could be placed on any of the findings. To give the exercise any credibility the correct definition of the angles of both the road alignment and the cadaster was vital; and that seemed to be an insuperable problem.

But a solution was at hand. Although the road alignment between Reagill and Scalesceugh was virtually 26°W of N, it had several sub-alignments that took the causeway westwards to the forts at Brougham and Old Penrith. I therefore needed to define the *mean* survey line and its inclination to see how it compared with the inclination of Itonfield Street. The solution was a statistical method to take account of the variation in the route of the causeway and of minor map reading errors. To understand it in context, a brief description of the road is needed. The 40-mile route from Low Borrowbridge to Carlisle has two main alignments; the first going due north from Low Borrowbridge to just south of Reagill Grange, and a second from thence to Carlisle. See Figure 2.8. In the middle of each alignment, sub-alignments take the causeway westwards before regaining the original line. Alignment 1, Low Borrowbridge to Reagill Grange, runs northwards along the OS grid meridian (easting 361.00). The first section is now lost beneath the motorway, but the road line runs to just north of Roundthwaite where, to avoid Orton Scar, it swings westward to Howeknowe Pike. It then turns to regain the meridian at the Iron Age settlement at Ewe Close. The two sub-alignments meet at an alignment node (OS 359.90 510.07) though the causeways meet by a curve. From Ewe Close, the road bears very slightly west to Reagill.

The shift to alignment 2 at Reagill is not upon a hilltop or any point of vantage from where a beacon might be seen. It is in the shallow valley of the Low Wood Beck where the view to the north is blocked by rising ground. Penrith Beacon Fell, a presumed survey point, cannot be seen until one is further north. There is no obvious topographical reason why this spot was chosen for the alignment shift. Alignment 2 leads off at about 25° W of N and runs for some five miles (The Street) to Gilshaughlin Wood, where the road swings further west to Brougham. The road then curves round Beacon Fell, straightens out and passing Old Penrith fort, makes for High Hesket where it falls in again with the alignment of the Street, i.e., directly on alignment 2. From High Hesket to Carleton, the road more or less holds to alignment 2, but at Gallows Hill, just south of Carlisle, it shifts slightly westward, leaving alignment 2 to pass east of the city to Stanwix.

Because for much of the way between Gilshaughlin Wood and High Hesket the road runs well to the west of alignment 2, one cannot be quite sure whether it was intentionally related to that alignment. This was where the statistical method came in. Linear regression is a statistical means of assessing to what extent two variables are correlated. The best example of the principle is the spring balance used to weigh vegetables. The length of the spring is directly proportional to the weight placed upon it, so plotting on a graph the spring's length

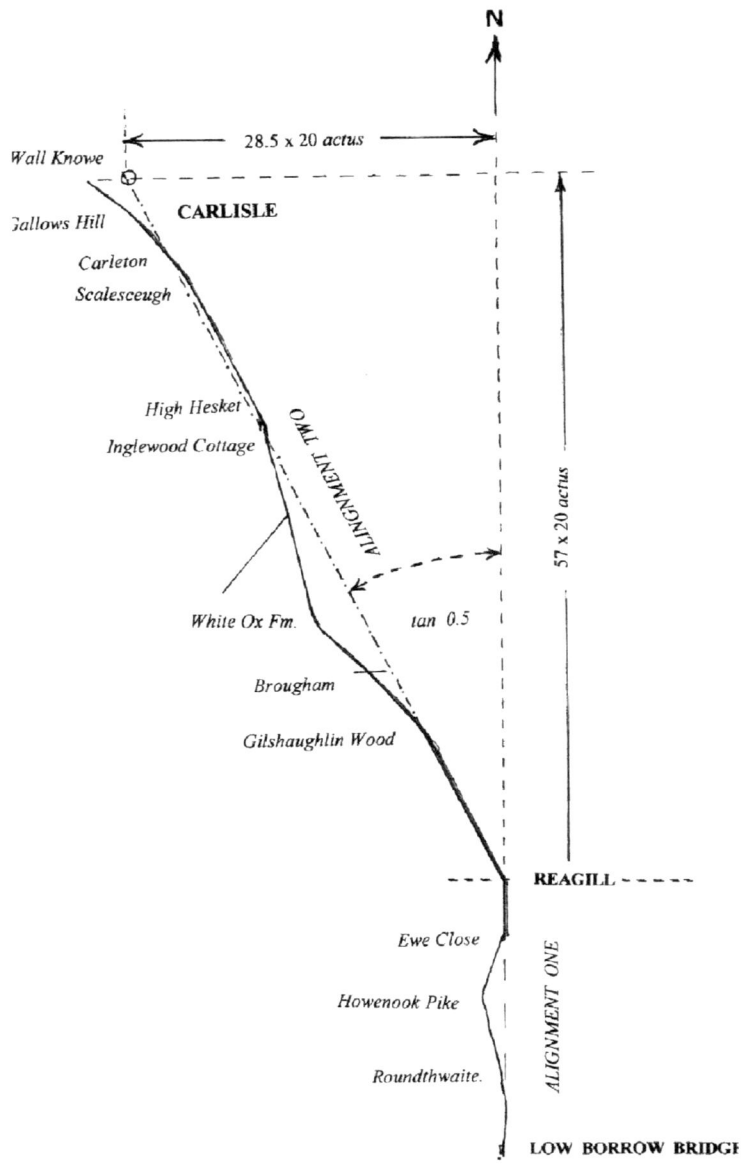

Figure 2.8: Reagill - Carlisle Roman road alignments: (After Ferrar & Richardson 2003)

against various weights gives a perfectly straight line. If, however, one were to plot the height of children against their ages, one would not get a perfect line because children vary; yet the overall statement that a child's height correlates with its age might still be true. Mathematicians have developed linear regression to deal with this problem. The details need not concern us, but the method finds the best straight line relating two data sets and tells us how close the correlation is. A *correlation coefficient* of 1.0 means the data points relate to a straight line. The nearer the coefficient is to 1.0, the better the fit. The *slope* is the angle that the line makes to the graph's axes and is expressed as the *Tangent* of the angle. Probability tables tell us to what extent the result is due to chance. It is thus an ideal method to define the angle of a set of OS grid reference points that appear to lie on a straight line i.e., the alignment nodes of a Roman road. The slope is much more reliable because it is based on all the data points; not just the two at each end of the alignment.

The correlation coefficient for all the nodes on alignment 2 proved to be 0.99; virtually a straight line and the chances that this was accidental were 1000 to 1 against; very highly significant. The calculation was done with a Microsoft Excel spreadsheet using the data given in Appendix 3. One could safely say that throughout its length, the road was intentionally related to alignment 2. The slope was precisely *Tan* 0.5, that is 1/2, W of N. The angle in degrees is 26.63°. Now this is a value of no significance whereas the Tangent 1/2, shows that in conceptual terms, the alignment is the hypotenuse of a right-angled triangle whose other two sides, in the ratio 1:2, are co-incident with the latitude and meridian. This was surely intentional.

Now, to connect two points by a line inclined to the OS meridian by an angle whose Tangent is an exact fraction (1/2), the road planners must have known the precise two-dimensional relationship of Reagill and Carlisle at the outset, and this could only have come from a scale plan upon which those points were spatially defined. Moreover, such a plan could only have been drawn after an accurate survey. Here, at last, was clear evidence of a level of surveying competence that went far beyond lighting beacons on the fells and fixing road alignments by inspired guesswork. Here was virtual proof of very sophisticated map-making. It did not produce the sort of modern map that describes the landscape in detail, but rather one that was very accurate for planning the infra-structure. The obvious question arising was how did the two cadasters tie-in with the putative map-grid and the road's design line?

Defining the inclination of cadaster B

Because linear regression offered a reliable means of defining an alignment angle from several data points, the Itonfield Street line was similarly examined. The data are set out in Appendix 4 and the results were equally eloquent; their precision being emphasised by the noughts in the decimal places; correlation coefficient = 1.00, and slope = 0.600 or 30.96°. Expressed as a fraction, 0.6 is 3/5. The angle in degrees is virtually 31°, just as with the cadaster at Florence. It meant that the *Itonfield Street* line was the hypotenuse of another right-angled triangle whose other sides were also along the latitude and the meridian, but in the ratio 3:5. The exercise was then performed with the grid references of the several small lanes between Middlesceugh Hall and Barrow Mill. The correlation coefficient was 0.999 and slope was 0.571 (32.7°). The small discrepancy in the slope is explained by these lanes being more scattered about the mean course than those along the Itonfield Street line. See Appendix 5.

These findings revealed that the Roman "blue-print" for this part of Cumbria comprised a grid aligned NS and EW (i.e. with lines longitude and latitude) to which the Hayton cadaster (A) was coincident but to which cadaster B was off-set in anti-clockwise manner. The Reagill-Carlisle road line related to the NSEW grid by an angle whose *Tangent* was ½ and cadaster B by one whose *Tangent* was 3/5. These angles are more correctly written Atan 1/2 and Atan 3/5.

This was a major breakthrough. The next step was to locate a point common to the road alignment and both cadasters; for this was likely to be the main survey datum point for the whole district.

A common datum point for the cadasters and the Reagill-Carlisle road line

The Middlesceugh Hall-Barrow Mill line lies 400 *actus* (20 *centuriae*) south of the Wall's crossing of the river. Eden. It intersects with Itonfield Street at OS 343.10 542.26 on *Street Field*, Low Braithwaite. The computer spreadsheet (Appendix 1) was now set to the precise angle, 30.96°, and used to pin-point other cadastral nodes exactly. Bearing in mind the Reagill-Carlisle road alignment passed east of Carlisle city, a node 20 *centuriae ultra* (above or northwards) and eight *centuriae dextra* (to the right, or eastwards) of the Street Field node, was found just east of the Stanwix fort, on a hillock called Wall Knowe (OS 340.67 557.35). After the advent of global positioning satellites, I found this spot was actually on Brampton Road, a short distance from the top of Wall Knowe but still a good vantage point.

Further calculations (Appendix 6) then showed that the road alignment from Reagill cut the Wall Knowe northing (557.35) just 30 metres west of the previously identified cadastral node at 340.64E. Thus, here the Inglewood *limites* and the mean road line coincided; the 30 metres discrepancy is insignificant. This point turns out to be 57 x 20 *actus* N and 28.5 x 20 *actus* W of the Reagill node, which is highly significant because it reveals that the *agrimensores*' unit defined the *Tangent* of alignment 2 (28.5/57 = 0.5, or ½).

Moreover, How Street, Hayton, running along northing 557.00, turns out to be 10 *actus*, or half a *centuria*, south of Wall Knowe and so neatly fits into this putative NSEW survey grid. These findings seemed to put beyond reasonable doubt that the two cadasters lay within a survey grid that had also defined the road alignment between Low Borrowbridge and Carlisle. But how far did this survey extend? A *tetrans* for the cadasters seemed more elusive than ever. Then I noticed that Wall Knowe was on the same meridian as the Roman fortress at Chester. Could it be that the survey covered the whole north of England?

Michael J Ferrar

While I had been thus occupied in Cumbria, unknown to me, Mr Michael Ferrar had been pursuing similar enquiries in the Midlands and the south of England. Being an architect and a competent draughtsman, he was able to draw lines accurately upon scale maps and overcome the problems that had defeated me. He was also a knowledgeable numerologist, familiar with ancient surveying and systems of measurement. He had already made several important observations on Roman roads and cadasters in southern England but had met the same stubborn resistance when it came to publishing his findings. We were put in touch by Professor Dilke and began to collaborate. His contribution to the final outcome of my Cumbrian studies was crucial and the synthesis of our work has been set out in our book.[29]
Among his many observations, Michael had made one that proved highly relevant to my Cumbrian findings and which confirmed beyond doubt that he had cracked the mystery of the Roman survey of Britain.

---

[29] Ferrar & Richardson (2003)

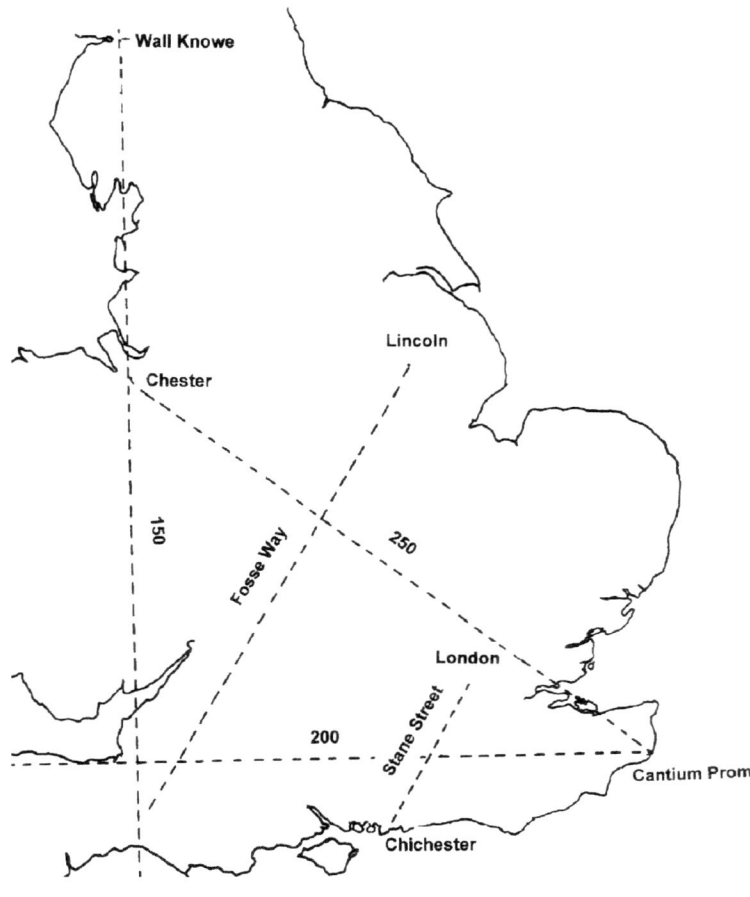

Figure 2.9: Some Roman survey lines in Britain: scale in Roman miles (After Ferrar & Richardson 2003)

When I informed Michael of the inclination angles of the cadasters and the road line, their relation to Wall Knowe and thus to the Chester fortress, he sent me several maps upon which he had marked out some astonishing geometrical relationships between Roman sites and roads throughout Britain. There were two that were immediately relevant to Cumbria; the inclinations of the Sussex Stane Street and the Fosse Way (Ilchester-Lincoln) were *Atan* 3/5 E of N, and Chester was related to the South Foreland at Dover, known to the Romans as *Cantium Prom*, by a Pythagorean right-angled triangle (sides in the ratio, 3, 4, 5) with a unitary dimension of 50 Roman miles; i.e., 150, 200, 250.[30] The NS distance between Wall Knowe and Chester was 130 Roman miles and the distance between Wall Knowe and the latitude of *Cantium Prom* was thus 280 Roman miles. Thus, my Cumbrian findings neatly fitted into Michael's scheme of a province-wide survey. See Figure 2.9.

Michael had established the major lines of this Roman survey grid, based on *Cantium Prom* and which embraced the whole province. He had found that many other Roman roads were related to the meridian and longitude by angles whose *Tangents* were simple fractions; this being due to their being defined in terms of the sides of a right-angled triangle whose non-hypotenuse sides were in whole number ratios. The reason for this peculiarity was almost certainly a consequence of the roads being planned upon a grid whereby their lines connected certain grid nodes. See Figure 2.10.

---

[30] Ferrar & Richardson (2003)

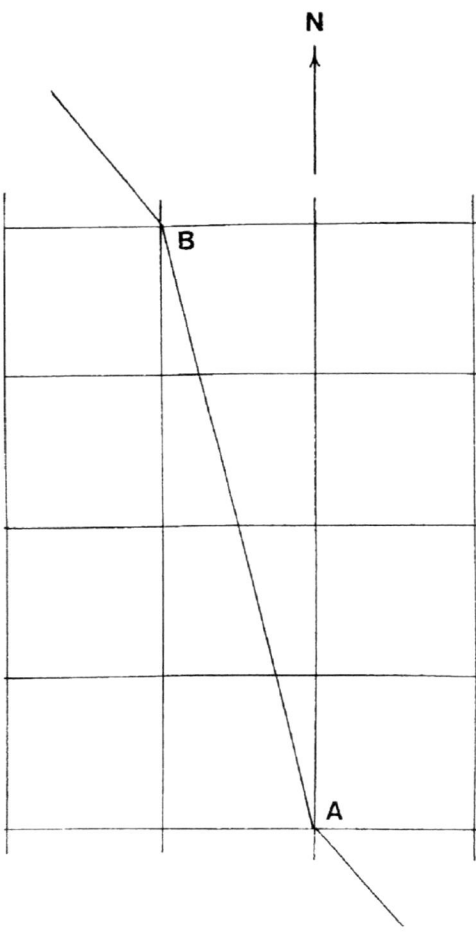

Figure 2.10:
Rational Tangents: Because A and B stand upon a grid node, the line inclines Atan 1/4 W of N

The Proof

Nevertheless, no matter the weight of evidence and no matter how plausible such a scheme might be on paper, it required a leap of imagination to accept a Roman survey of this magnitude. We needed some sort of independent proof. We found one as a consequence of dealing with the criticism that on the OS map the NS grid-line is not necessarily the same as the true meridian. The difference is a consequence of the way maps are made and to understand it, it is necessary to say something of map projections; a subject with which Greek and Roman map-makers were quite familiar.[31]

Maps must be flat, but the earth is round. The Greeks knew this, though they took the earth to be a perfect sphere whereas we know it is flattened towards the poles and has some unevenness elsewhere. From the spherical model they drew a number of logical conclusions. Lines of latitude are parallel, but lines of longitude converge towards the poles. Therefore a degree of latitude, in terms of NS distance on the earth's surface, is constant, whereas the further north we go from the equator each degree of longitude describes a shorter EW distance. Thus, on maps of large areas there is a problem with scale because the EW dimension is not constant. At its northern (top) end, in the northern hemisphere, it is decreased. At any

---

[31]Dilke (1985)

point on earth's surface there is a particular ratio of distance per degree longitude to that of latitude and the ancients knew this to be the *Cosine* of the latitude: 1.[32]

To deal with this problem when mapping large areas, Claudius Ptolemy (c. AD 90 - 168), in his first projection, regarded the northern hemisphere as a cone with straight, rather than curved, longitudinal lines.[33] But we must remember that he was drawing on the work of several distinguished predecessors active before the Roman conquest of Britain. This projection was reasonable for large-scale maps but it meant that a rectangular map still suffered EW distortion. But for most practical purposes, this distortion was negligible. For mapping "prefectures and provinces" wrote Ptolemy, "...nor will it make much difference if in these maps we use parallel meridian straight lines instead of curved lines, provided we keep the proper proportion of the meridian degrees marked on...to those in the middle of every map."[34] In effect, he advised surveyors to find the province's mid-latitude and mid-longitude and then adjust the longitudinal (EW) distances to those at to the mid latitude for the whole map. This produced a flat map with a rectangular grid whose longitude lines were closer together than the latitudinal lines, but with the *appropriate proportion*, noted on the map. For example at 60° N the *Cosine* of the latitude is 0.5, so the lines of longitude would be spaced at intervals that were half of the latitude intervals. The resulting map would have parallel longitudes but at the northern edge they would be *outside* the converging, true longitudes and inside them at the bottom. For relatively small regional maps this was not, as Ptolemy wrote, a major problem.

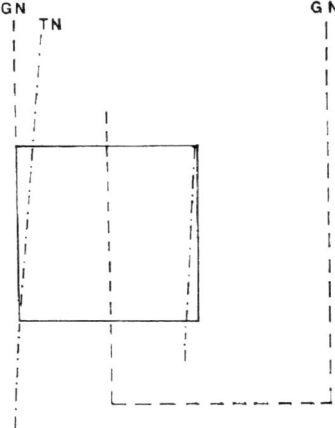

Figure 2.11: The relationship of Grid North (GN) to the True North (TN) on an orthogonal map grid

The Ordnance Survey dealt with the problem in the same way. They chose for the mid longitude of Britain the meridian 2° W of Greenwich, running from Poole Harbour through Berwick upon Tweed. This line was made N for the whole map, which was then marked with a regular orthogonal grid. This was based on Grid N but calibrated from an origin in the sea beyond the Scilly Isles, such that the mid longitude was at 400E. The difference between grid N and true N is scarcely detectable for several miles either side of easting 400 but it is noticeable in the eastern and western parts of the country.

---

[32] Harley & Woodward (1987, 141)
[33] Dilke (1985, 78)
[34] Stephenson (1932, prologue)

West of OS 400E, true N inclines eastwards (1.5° in West Wales, about 0.8° at Carlisle) while east of it, true N it inclines westwards (2.53° in East Norfolk). Northings, overlying latitudes, pose no problem. This is shown in Figure 2.11 which shows the relationship of Grid North to the meridian, or True N, on a map covering an area west of the mid longitude. Thus, Roman surveyors using sundials to find the directions of meridian and latitude at Carlisle would not define a NS line that coincided with that of our OS map. They would indeed find the true meridian, but it would be inclined about 0.8° east of the OS Grid N line. How, then, could Itonfield Street be inclined exactly *Atan* 3/5 W of OS grid N, and the main road line inclined exactly at *Atan* 1/2? If these angles had been set out to the locally determined meridian, the Itonfield Street line would have been 30.96 - 0.8 = 30.16°, and the road (alignment 2) would have been 26.63 - 0.8 = 25.83°. The discrepancies are small but the angles determined by linear regression were unequivocal and statistically very sound. Remember, the slope for the points along the Itonfield Street line was 0.600; zeros to the third decimal place. The only explanation is that the Roman map grid had its mid-longitude very close to OS 400E.

TABLE 2.1: TANGENTS OF ALIGNMENT ANGLES TO THE MERIDIAN AND TO OS GRID NORTH
(After Ferrar and Richardson 2003)

	Tangent as a rational fraction	
	Meridian	*OS grid North*
Norfolk *limites*	77/500	1/5
Peddar's Way, Norfolk	187/500	3/7
Cumberland *limites*	31/50	3/5
Reagill - Carlisle road	26/50	1/2
Honiton - Exeter road	100/47 approx	9/4

This conclusion is supported by evidence from elsewhere, for if the hypothesis be true, the Tangents to grid N and local true N, of Roman roads in the east and west of Britain should differ; with roads relating to the OS grid by angles with simpler, i.e. more accurate, fractional Tangents than those to the local meridian. This comparison was made for alignments in Cumbria, Devon and East Anglia, using the deviation of true N given on the relevant OS map sheets. The results are shown in Table 2.1. There can be no doubt that the simpler rational fractions relate to OS grid N rather than to the local meridian. Indeed one might almost say that the Tangents relating to true N are not rational fractions at all, since they stretch the definition of that term to breaking point.

Conclusion

This state of affairs can only mean that across the whole country the Romans used the same grid whose N coincided with true N at some chosen mid-longitude of the country. It follows that this must have been about OS 400E. The fact that the Reagill - Carlisle road alignments (and some others) formed the hypotenuses of triangles, whose other sides were multiples of 20 *actus*, indicate that the grid was of 20 *actus* squares, the standard agrimensorial type.

It now remains to see how the Roman map was probably made.

PART THREE

THE ROMAN SURVEY OF BRITAIN

Historic background

Before the days of Herodotus (490-425 BC) several Greek geographers had postulated that the earth was a sphere. They then used mathematics to tackle the problem of measuring its dimensions; i.e. geometry, literally "measuring the earth". Eratosthenes (*circa* 275-194 BC) calculated the circumference to be 250,000 *stades*,[1] but later modified it to 252,000 *stades*. He observed that at the summer solstice, the sun shone straight down a well at Aswan on the upper Nile whilst casting a shadow at Alexandria. He measured the shadow angle carefully and relied on a measurement of the distance between the latitudes of the two places. He almost certainly worked in terms of the Egyptian *stade* of 157.8 metres; so in Roman measure his circumference was 26,893 miles, or 27,000 in round figures; not far off the true value. This gave a distance of 74.7, say, 75 miles per degree of latitude and it seems that the Romans, who were intrigued by numerical niceties, liked this. Pliny thought the dimension had divine approval.[2] Moreover, the value of 27,000 miles might have been similarly appreciated, 27 being 3 cubed. The ancients could not imagine that nature might throw up awkward numbers; that was not how the gods worked.

The Greeks, as we have noted, knew that whilst lines of latitude are parallel, lines of longitude converge towards the poles, where all meet, and they deduced that at any point of the earth's surface, the relationship of longitude to latitude was *Cosine* latitude to 1. They then calculated the ratio for several places. Eratosthenes, presumably relying on information from travellers such as Pytheas of Marseilles who visited Britain about the year 300 BC, placed Britain between 50° N and 62° N, with its mid-latitude at 56°[3] N. Here, the latitude-longitude ratio was 0.56, or in fractional terms 11:20, the very ratio later recommended by Claudius Ptolemy for the British map.

The evidence reported in the last chapter suggests that the problem of making a flat map of the earth's curved surface was solved long before Claudius Ptolemy wrote of "his" conical projection; a conclusion drawn by other scholars. Ptolemy noted that "his" projection would create problems with scale for maps of large areas, though not for a "regional map" because the distance per degree of latitude and longitude would depend on the estimate of the earth's circumference. Using Eratosthenes's data the distance per degree longitude in Britain would be 0.56 x 75 = 42 Roman miles and so the map would have parallel latitudes marked at 75-mile intervals and parallel lines of longitude at 42-mile intervals, but with the proportion indicated on the map. But Posidonius (circa. 150-135 BC) complicated matters by calculating the earth's circumference to be 180,000 *stades* (much smaller) and in the early second century AD Claudius Ptolemy accepted this. But by then, Britain was mapped and the evidence points to the Roman surveyors of Britain having worked to the model of Eratosthenes, with one degree of latitude equalling 75 Roman miles.

---

[1] Diller (1948, 7)

[2] Diller (1948, 7)

[3] Gossellin (1883)

[4] Harley and Woodward (1987, 130 - 148)

[5] Stevenson (1932)

By the time of the invasion of AD 43, the Romans had plenty of information on Britain derived from Julius Caesar, spies and, presumably, the Greek academic corpus. They probably had the recently published work of Strabo (*circa* 63 BC-23 AD) from whom they would have learned that Britain was triangular in outline with one point, known as *Cantium Prom*, at the narrowest part of the Channel.[6] This was the South Foreland near Dover where Julius Caesar reported that ships from the continent usually landed.[7] Roman merchants would be familiar with the south coast and almost certainly the army staff had the latitudes determined by Pytheas. In short, they were far better informed than the grotesquely corrupted map attributed to Claudius Ptolemy would suggest.

The establishment of the mid longitude

After the landing, a military surveying team almost certainly began a new survey. The first aim would be to establish a base line from which to determine the mid-longitude and mid-latitude of the island, or at least that portion intended for the province. *Cantium Prom* could be linked directly to Gaul and was an obvious starting point. The meridian would be found by sundial and a line, marked out at right angles (using the Pythagorean 3:4:5 triangle) could be made to stretch westwards along the latitude (OS 143.30N). This line would be marked by a series of posts and by viewing across their tops and checking the alignment by sundial at noon, the surveyors could maintain a high degree of accuracy. They probably progressed at about 12 miles a day, as in marching, and in a little over three weeks they would have reached the west coast. The line was probably measured in 12 Roman-mile units, since this distance is 60,000 (12 x 5000) Roman feet, or 500 *actus*, or 25 *centuriae*. Note how a 12-Roman-mile unit neatly fits with agrimensorial measure. Oddly, this parallel happens to be the longest EW line available across southern Britain, just skirting the north coast of Devon to finish at Woolacombe. A line a little further north would have ended at Burnham on Sea, 60 miles to the east on the Somerset coast, and a line further south would have had to start at Romney Marsh. The two lines are of similar length, but the Dover parallel is much longer.

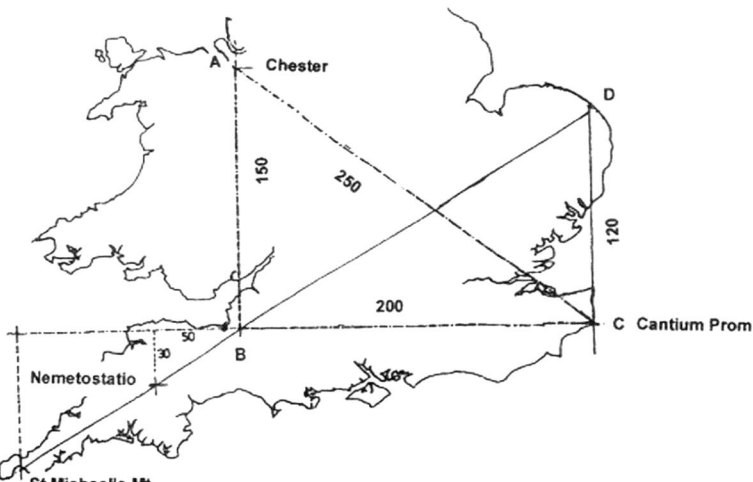

Figure 3.1: Putative Roman survey lines in SW England: units are Roman miles (After Ferrar & Richardson 2003)

---

[6] Aujac (1987, 174)
[7] Handford (1951, 135)

Somewhere about the mid point of this base line, they would fix the mid-longitude of the province. The choice was not straightforward because of the south-west peninsula, but the problem was almost certainly resolved by extending the survey into Devon and Cornwall. Although we cannot be certain about how this was done, we can suggest a possibility. Two observation are relevant; the location of the Roman fort, known as *Nemetostatio*, at North Tawton in Devon and the Wall Knowe - Chester meridian (OS 340.60E) that we have already met. The latter turns out to be 200 Roman miles west of *Cantium Prom* and it intersects with the survey's putative EW base line at a point just west of Salisbury Plain. From there, the location of *Nemetostatio* is defined by a 3:5 right-angled triangle, such that the fort bears Atan 3/5 S of W. Moreover, the relevant dimensions are 50 Roman miles west and 30 south; an extraordinary co-incidence if it were not designed that way. When the direct line (hypotenuse) is projected, it reaches a point close to St Michaels Mount (OS 029.90N) which turns to be 75 Roman miles south of *Cantium Prom*, or one degree of latitude (Eratosthenes), remarkable co-incidence. See Figure 3.1. By measuring to this point and knowing the properties of the 3:5 right-angled triangle, they would calculate that the Mount stood 125 miles west of the post standing 200 miles west of *Cantium Prom*. See Appendix 7 for the explanation.

So, the EW distance between *Cantium Prom* and the datum point near St Michael's Mount was 325 miles. Its halfway point would be 162.5 miles west of *Cantium Prom* but it so happens that 160 Roman miles west is OS 399.51E, within half a km. of the OS grid N, (400.00E) and the Roman surveyors probably chose this for the mid longitude because it kept their figures simple. This would explain why the Roman grid is almost indistinguishable from the OS grid. See Figure 3.2.

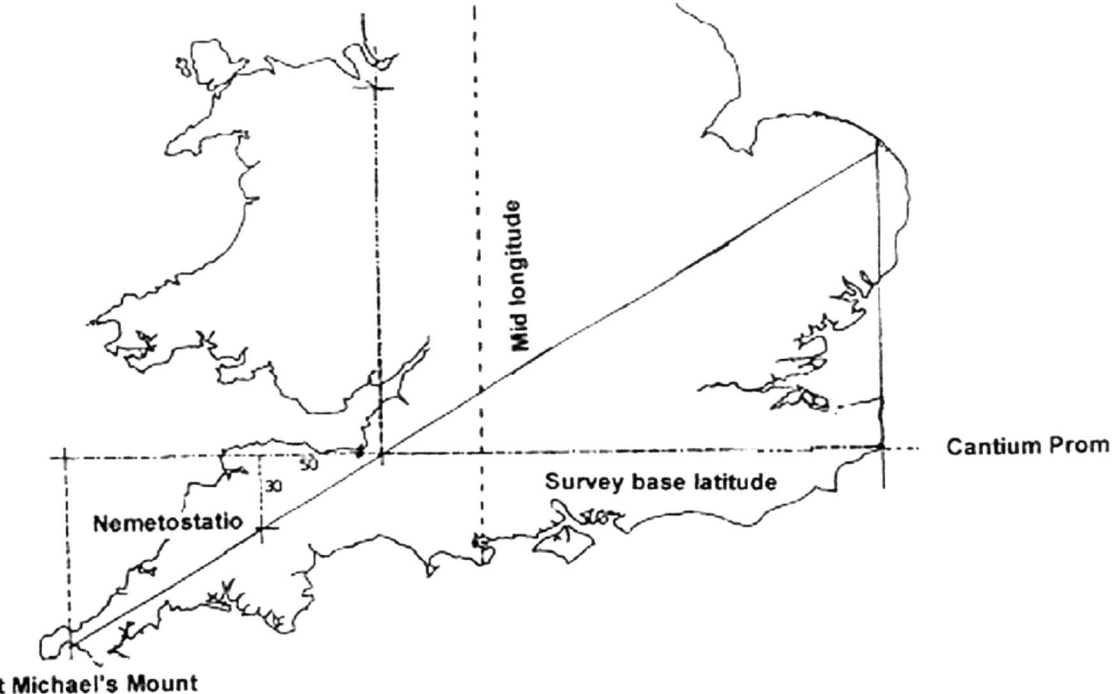

Figure 3.2: The putative Roman mid longitude: units = Roman miles (After Ferrar & Richardson 2003)

Having selected the mid-longitude, another line of posts would be driven northwards and southwards along it, accuracy being constantly checked by sundial. Secondary lines would then be pegged out parallel to the main survey lines, just as in centuriation. The expanding grid would thus define the spatial relationships of native towns and natural features and permit the drawing of accurate and practically useful maps, or *formae*, complete with co-ordinates. The planning of roads thus became a relatively simple matter of setting design lines across the country by connecting survey grid nodes. The engineers could make necessary local amendments for the line of the causeway. There was no need for primitive devices such hill-top beacons, except where their location had *first* been carefully determined from the *forma*.

The probable mid latitude

Ptolemy's map making method, which it must be repeated was probably in use before his time, required the province's mid latitude to be found so that the latitude-longitude ratio could be calculated. Chester cathedral, on the longitude of Wall Knowe stands on the site of the Roman fortress and is 150.8 miles north of the EW base line at OS 366.60N. This is virtually 2 x 75 = 150 Roman miles, which on Eratosthenes's model would be two degrees of latitude. Therefore the actual datum was probably 0.8 miles (4,000 feet) south of the fortress (OS 365.10N) making the right-angled triangle formed between *Cantium Prom*, the Chester datum point and the grid node already identified west of Salisbury Plain (OS 340.60 143.30). It is the classic Pythagorean 3:4:5 triangle with units of 50 Roman miles; 150: 200: 250. See Figure 3.1. It seems very likely that the position of the Chester fortress was chosen with the aid of the map and intended to be as near as possible to the mid-latitude of the province, if not the island.

Chester may also have been intended as the main provincial survey office. Within the fortress was an enigmatic building of elliptical outline and monumental proportions. It had bays, suggestive of a library, but it was never finished and is known only from its foundations and unfinished walls. It appears very suitable for a land registry and survey archive and it happens that Sextus Julius Frontinus, author of several surveying texts preserved in the *Corpus Agrimensorum Romanorum*, was the governor active at Chester at the time of the building's inception. He may have intended the elliptical building as agrimensorial data base, but if so, his plan was abandoned for the building was never completed.

Wall Knowe is 130.0 Roman miles north of the Chester datum. This supports the idea that the survey grid was used to fix secondary survey datum points, like Wall Knowe, from which cadasters and road alignments were then planned. At Manchester, such a survey point probably existed where Piccadilly railway station now stands, for all seven Roman roads approaching the fort appear to be aligned on it.[8]

A final observation on the peculiar importance the Romans attached to the significance of one degree of latitude (Eratosthenes), or 75 Roman miles, concerns the frontier wall of Hadrian and that of Antoninus Pius in Scotland. The difference between the mean latitudes of the two walls, when calculated from the OS northings of their forts, is exactly 75 Roman miles.[9]

The accuracy of the survey

The evidence points to the *agrimensores* having worked to a very high standard. It is, of course, impossible to carry out surveys, or any form of measurement, without some error, but the *groma*, though a simple instrument, could be used to great effect. It had a most significant feature, the arm or bracket, which connected the upright staff to the cross-arms. Fabricius (1901) reconstructed one from the information given in the *Corpus Agrimensorum* and

---

[8] Richardson (2004 a, 65 - 66)

[9] Ferrar & Richardson (2003, 63 - 68)

concluded that this arm enabled the axis of the off-set cross-piece to be placed exactly above the datum peg from which the measurements were to be made. Della Corte (1912) discovered at Pompeii several metal fittings that he identified as the furnishings of a *groma* and his reconstructed instrument had an off-set arm 2.5 cm long. This can only mean that such an instrument was intended for land measurements accurate to the inch. However, Schioler (1994) has denied that *gromae* were furnished with such arms and to support his view cited their absence on two tombstones. The point may therefore be in dispute, but all the evidence, especially that from the Inglewood centuriation and the Carlisle - Reagill road, indicates that Roman surveyors worked to a very high standard.

Discussion

In summary, the first surveying objectives after the invasion were to define an EW base line and to establish the mid-longitude; just as Claudius Ptolemy later recommended, as if he had first thought of it. The surveyors probably defined the line by posts and measured the distances in Roman miles. They chose the mid-longitude at 160 miles west of *Cantium Prom*. A second line was then set out to the north and south along this mid longitude. The next phase saw the setting out of tertiary survey lines from the two base lines to make an orthogonal grid. Early in the process, the Fosse Way was set out *Atan* 3/5 E of N from a point on the mid longitude near Cirencester [10]. As the grid extended across the country, the map (*forma*) would be composed square by square. The country south of the Chester parallel was probably surveyed in the first phase, with that to north in the second. The beauty of this system was that a large, clumsy map was not necessary; a matrix of lines could define the whole, or any part thereof, at any desired scale. After the survey, any medium bearing a grid could be used to make an accurate sketch map and doubtless the army used them for both campaigns and policing. Moreover, the whole country could be described as a series of squares, and squares within squares, which would have made documentation and archiving quite straightforward.

The map of Roman Britain known to us as Claudius Ptolemy's map, and which is so grotesque as to be a joke, is in fact a construction based on the estimated latitudes and longitudes of several places listed in his *Geographia*. This work was re-discovered as a 12th century text during the Renaissance, when it was re-published. There can be little doubt that the several copyings made during the previous 1,000 years resulted in an accumulation of errors in the numerical data. The reconstructed map must be dismissed as a serious reflection on Ptolemy's abilities and the achievements of the ancient Greek cartographers.

The putative Roman map grid described above may be drawn upon the Ordnance Survey map using the eastings and northings at 10 Roman-mile intervals from *Cantium Prom* given in Appendix 8. It is almost certain that further studies of the Romano-British landscape made in the context of this grid will reveal hitherto unsuspected Roman features and will shed new light on established ones. For example, road lines that are suspected of being Roman, but for which there is little conventional supporting evidence. Indeed, as we shall see in Part Five, certain roads, never remotely suspected of having a Roman origin, may come into focus.

***

---

[10] Ferrar & Richardson (2003, 3 - 5)

PART FOUR

CUMBERLAND REVISITED

Roman roads at Carlisle

The realisation that the Reagill-Carlisle Roman road alignment and the cadasters were based on a province-wide survey lead to another observation; that Carlisle showed certain characteristics of the classical Greek town plan often adopted by the Romans. This plan was also based on a *decumanus* and a *kardo* set at right angles and aligned on the cardinal points; *kardo* EW and *decumanus* NS. The two main streets normally overlay each axis, at least as far as the city gates and often for a short distance beyond.[1] Three major roads approaching Carlisle, two accepted as Roman, lie on the cardinal points. See Figure 4.1.

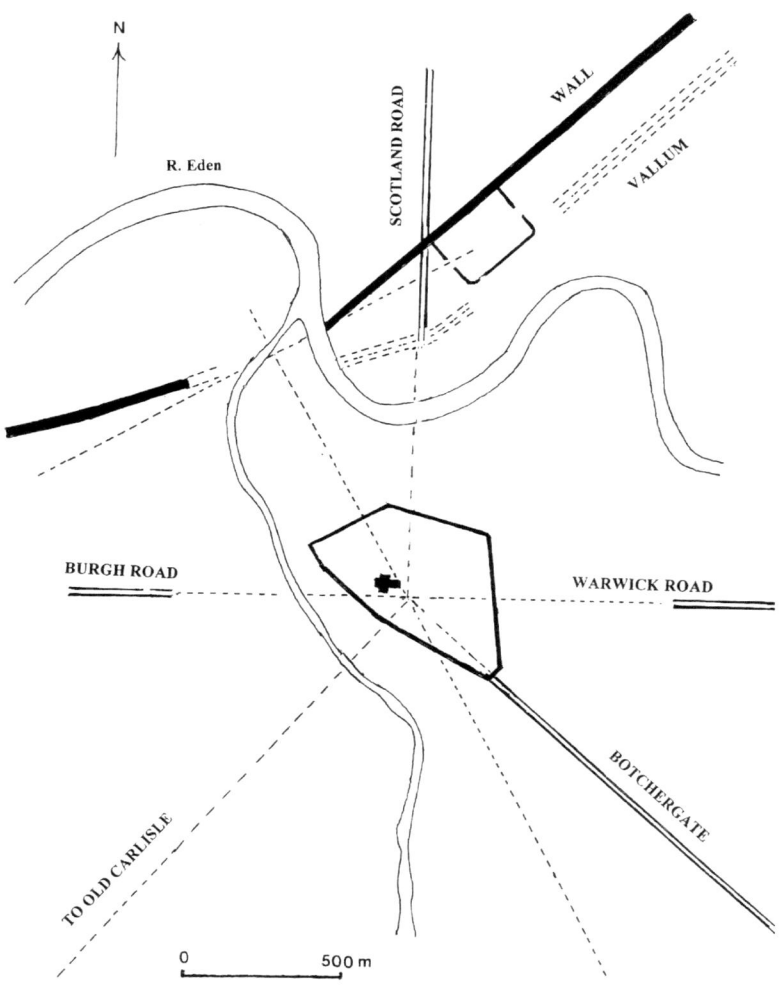

Figure 4.1: Roman road alignments at Carlisle: Scale = 500 m.

From the North: Scotland Road, whose Roman precursor (about OS 339.90E) ran some 50 metres west of the modern road.[2,3]

---

[1] Dilke (1971, 86-87)
[2] Hogg (1952)
[3] Caruana & Coulson (1987)

From the West: Burgh Road (OS 555.90N) almost certainly overlying the last section of the Stanegate coming from the Kirkbride fort.[4]

From the East: The main line of Warwick Road, east of the bend at Hartington Place, also follows OS northing 555.90, which is 4,900 feet south of Wall Knowe. This probably means that its Roman precursor was actually *two centuriae* (4,800 feet) south of that survey point; the discrepancy, given the map scale, being insignificant. There is no immediate evidence of Warwick Road continuing eastwards on a Roman line, but the bridge at Warwick was mentioned in 1170 [5] and 1260 [6] and in 1455 certain nearby fields were described in relation to the *alta via*, the high road.[7] It is therefore highly likely that a Roman road left Carlisle going eastwards.

From the South: Botchergate, representing the final sub-alignment of the road from Brougham, enters the Roman city at an angle of *Atan* 5/4 W of N [8], probably because the area immediately south of the city is occupied by the river Caldew.

The projected road alignments from north, east and west meet at OS 339.90 555.90, a point within the cathedral precincts and probably within the forum of the Roman city. Given the scale errors inherent in reading the map, the true datum is likely to have been defined from Wall Knowe by the agrimensorial units of 4,800 feet (40 *actus*) and 2,400 feet (20 *actus*). This point appears to have been the *tetrans* of cadaster A.

Cadaster A

Several other observations suggest that cadaster A had its KM on the Warwick Road - Burgh Road line; its DM on the Roman precursor of Scotland Road, and extended well to the east and west of the city. Between Carlisle and Kirkbride, many modern field boundaries and roads are aligned NSEW, such that the general pattern of later enclosure fits the grid. See Figure 4.2. Significantly, there are at least five villages whose main streets, running NS, stand at multiples of *centuriae* from *tetrans* A, and there are three similar to the east. Table 4.1 numbers them as *decumani*, according to their distance from *tetrans* A, i.e., D1W or D2E.

To the west, the main streets of Great Orton, Oughterby and Lessonhall appear to mark *quintariae,* since they occur at five *centuria* intervals. On the east Fenton Gate, Hayton, (15 *centuriae*) and the mean line of the road north from Castle Carrock (20 *centuriae*) also appear to represent *quintariae*. There is an apparent *decumanus* (D6E) at Scotby. The road south from Carlisle through Blackwell to Durdar, not listed in Table 4.1, roughly follows the meridian OS 340.25E and straddles a line 10 *actus* (1/2 *centuria*) east of *tetrans* A. It may represent a mid-centurial track (D0.5W). At Durdar it crosses Newbiggin Road (OS 551N), at right-angles.

---

[4] Bellhouse & Richardson (1982)
[5] Armstrong et al (undated, 151)
[6] Armstrong et al (undated, 163)
[7] Gray (1959, 324)
[8] Ferrar & Richardson (2003, 70)

TABLE 4.1: DISTANCES OF CERTAIN VILLAGE STREETS (ALIGNED N-S) FROM CARLISLE CATHEDRAL

Village	OS reference	Distance from Carlisle *tetrans* (OS 339.90E)		
		metres	*actus*	*centuriae*
West				
Great Orton	332.85	7,110	200.2	10.0 (D10W)
Oughterby	329.30	10,660	300.1	15.0 (D15W)
Aikton	327.90	12,460	350.8	17.5
Kirkbride	323.00	16,910	476.1	23.8
Lessonhall	322.15	17,760	500.0	25.0 (D25W)
East				
Scotby	344.20	4,290	120.8	6.0 (D6E)
Fenton Gate	350.60	10,690	301.0	15.0 (D15E)
Brampton Street	352.70	12,800	360.4	18.0 (D18E)
Castle Carrock	354.15	14,240	400.0	20.0 (D20E)

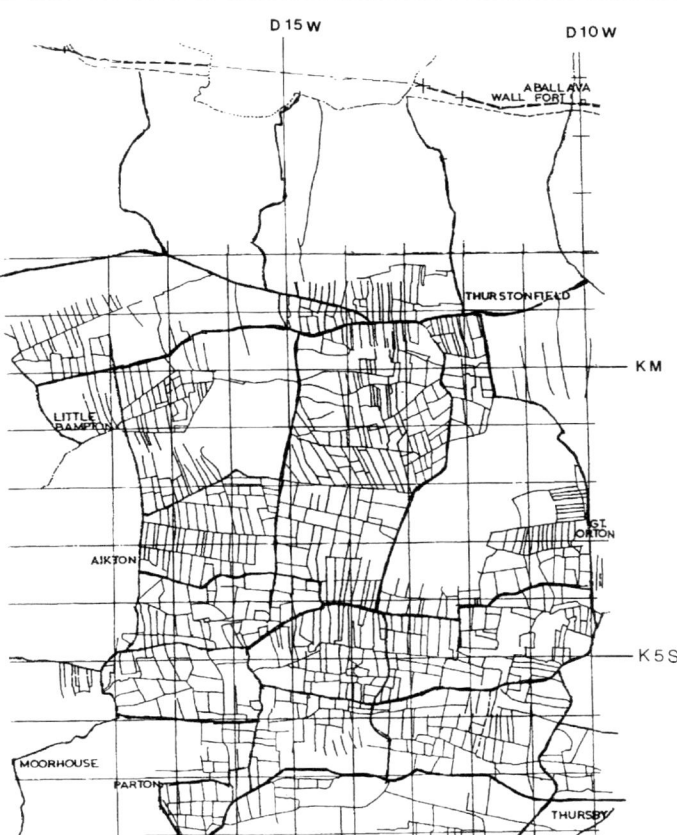

Figure 4.2: Lanes and field boundaries at Aikton in relation to cadaster A limites

[9] Brampton Street is mentioned in a description of Carlattan bounds in 1613 (Graham 1920, 9). Its precise location is not clear and it might be identified with the "street coming from Armathwaite" mentioned by Graham 1905). Mr Paul Wilson of Lorton, a careful antiquary, concluded in a letter to Mr R.L Bellhouse that it ran due south from Two Top, the end southern end of Thief Street, to the site of Carlattan's now lost church at Hall's Tenement. If this is so, it marked D18W (A) as shown in the table. Certain items of Mr Wilson's correspondence with Mr Bellhouse are preserved in Dr T.M. Allan's papers in Tullie House, Carlisle.

There is also evidence of certain village main streets overlying *kardines*, i.e. EW lines. See Table 4.2. The *limes* K1N is represented at Kirkbampton, while to the south, K1S runs through Little Orton and Little Bampton; and K4S through Wiggonby. Newbiggin Road fits K7S. However, How Street and Hayton's main village street, though one *centuria* apart, occur at half-*centuria* intervals within the cadaster, suggesting that here intra-centurial tracks were perhaps better preserved; perhaps by later settlements. In a *cadaster* at Manchester, there is evidence of roads through the middle of each alternate *centuria*, i.e., at 30 *actus* intervals.[10] Such an arrangement here could account for Aikton standing 17.5 *centuriae* to the west (Table 4.1). The EW alignment of the B6264 road west of Brampton would overlie K6N.

Given the observational error inherent in working with maps at this scale, these findings are remarkable. The *centuria* is 2,400 Roman feet, so a whole number multiple testifies to the strength of the data. They suggest that cadaster A extended from the coast near Kirkbride to the river Gelt, a breadth of 44 *centuriae*. Newbiggin Road appears to be its southern limit, with the northern limit at the latitude of Kirkbampton. The eastings and northings of the *quintariae* of cadaster A are given at Appendix 9.

TABLE 4.2: DISTANCES OF CERTAIN VILLAGE STREETS (ALIGNED E-W) FROM CARLISLE CATHEDRAL

Village	OS reference	Distance from Carlisle *tetrans* (OS 555.90N)		
North		metres	*actus*	*centuriae*
B6264 at Crosby Moor	560.15	4250	120	6 (K6N)
Hayton main street	557.70	1800	51	2.5
How Street	557.00	1100	31	1.5
Kirkbampton	556.60	700	20	1.0 (K1N)
South				
Oughterby	555.70	110	3.1	0.2
Little Orton	555.20	710	20.0	1.0 (K1S)
Little Bampton	555.20	710	20.0	1.0 (K1S)
Wiggonby	553.05	2860	80.5	4.0 (K4S)
Gamelsby	552.83	3525	99.2	5.0 (K5S)
Newbiggin Road	550.95	4950	139.3	7.0 (K7S)
Lessonhall	552.38	5710	160.8	8.0 (K8S)

A singular observation suggests that cadaster A may have been intended to extend as far south as Greystoke. Mabil cross, or Mable Cross (OS 339.87 534.70) was a monument that once stood on the boundary of the Inglewood Forest with the manor of Greystoke. It was mentioned in the earliest account of the Forest but its provenance is not known and the site is now a newly planted wood.[11] It was one of many ancient crosses of unknown provenance that dot our landscape, often in obscure places. Michael Ferrar and I have speculated that at least some of these monuments stand upon Roman survey points, with the cross explained by Christian generations super-imposing a holy symbol to expunge any pagan association,

---

[10] Richardson (2004 a)

[11] The Ordnance Survey, English Heritage and the Cumbria Sites and Monuments Record Office were unable to give any information on Mabil Cross. The late Dr T.M. Allan suggested in correspondence that it may have

especially where inscriptions had invoked the gods of the *agrimensores*.[12] A legend refers to St Paulinus banishing a heathen deity in a similar act of piety and placing a cross on Cross Fell, above Kirkland.[13] Interestingly, a point 40 *centuriae* (800 *actus*) due east of Mabil Cross is just below the NW corner of the scarp of Cross Fell.[14]

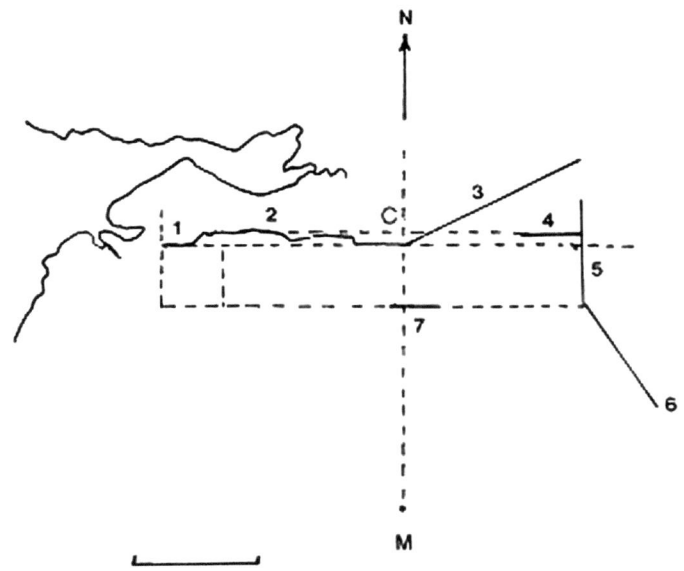

Figure 4.3: Cadaster A and associated roads: (1) Kirkbride (2) Kirkbampton (C) Carlisle (3) mean line of Stanegate (4) How Street (5) Castle Carrock (6) Appleby Street (7) Newbiggin Road (M) Mabil Cross (Scale = 7 miles)

However, Mabil Cross stood on the meridian of *tetrans* A (OS 339.875E); the 30-metre discrepancy being negligible at the 1:25,000 map scale. See Figure 4.3. This is curious; but even more curious is the fact that the intervening distance is 600 *actus* (30 *centuriae*). This observation is consistent with Mabil Cross having stood upon a Roman survey beacon that marked the intended terminus of the *decumanus maximus* of cadaster A. Such a cadaster would have had an area of 32 x 44 = 1,408 *centuriae*, though the evidence cited above suggests that only the northern parts were ever centuriated. The failure to complete the task may be explained by the advent of cadaster B which was superimposed over its middle portion.

Cadaster B

Although the location of cadaster B's *tetrans* is not immediately obvious, two possibilities present themselves; the provincial survey point at Wall Knowe and a point (T) two *centuriae* along a line *Atan* 3/5 S of W of it, at the Eden - Caldew confluence. A line from T perpendicular to that from Wall Knowe, passes very close to *tetrans* A. The relationship of these points is illustrated in Figure 4.4.

---

[12] Ferrar & Richardson (2003, 73-74)

[13] Whellan (1860)

[14] It may be significant that a survey point on Cross Fell due east of Mabil Cross would complete a Pythagorean triangle, (tetrans A, Mabil Cross, Cross Fell) with sides in the ratio 3:4: 5. The dimensions are 600, 800 and 1000 *actus*.

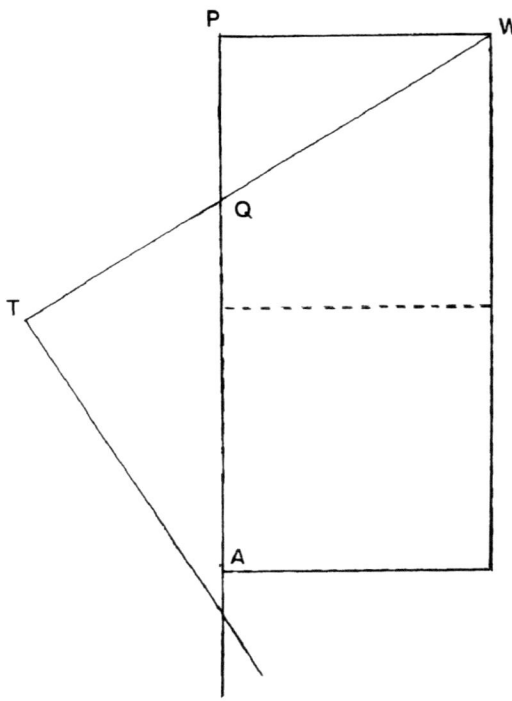

Figure 4.4: Survey lines at Carlisle: W = Wall Knowe: T = Confluence of Eden and Caldew; A = Cathedral: Scale: PW = 20 *actus*

At first sight cadaster B appears to result from cadaster A being rotated anti-clockwise through Atan 3/5, but this is deceptive. When a tracing paper ruled with a grid is laid over the map with a pin through *tetrans* A and then rotated anti-clockwise, the new grid does not overlie the *limites* of cadaster B. On the other hand if the exercise is repeated with the pin at Wall Knowe, the two grids do align. However, the DM of cadaster A could have been used in setting out the DM of cadaster B by the method suggested in Appendix 10. It seems likely that KM (B) originated at Wall Knowe but the prior existence of cadaster A invited its use in setting out DM (B), which for religious reasons may have had to traverse the Roman city. Cadaster B is also related geometrically through Wall Knowe to the Low Borrowbridge - Carlisle Roman road. The latter's alignment from Reagill is inclined *Atan* 1/2 rather than *Atan* 3/5 W of N, and though these figures suggest a large difference, in terms of degrees it is only 4.33 °; (30.96-26.63).

It is now necessary to number the cadaster B *limites* so as to relate them to significant landscape features. If we presume the observer stands at the rivers' confluence, facing south, the *decumani* to the right are west, whilst those to the left are east. Thus, the Itonfield Street line, the eighth from Wall Knowe, becomes D6W. This is not a *quintarius*, though it appears to have been a relatively substantial *limes*. On the other hand, the Skelton-Middlesceugh line (D10W) is a *quintarius* and for that reason may have been sufficiently well preserved to have been used early in the enclosure process. There is no evidence of cadaster B *limites* north of the Wall, so all *kardines* are south.

Now certain of those mysterious ancient roads and streets mentioned in the historic record may be identified as *limites*, at least tentatively. See Table 4.3.

TABLE 4.3: SOME HISTORICALLY RECORDED FEATURES WITHIN CADASTER B

Feature	Reference	Probable *limes*
Old pack horse road, Aiketgate	Wilson (1976)	D3E
Via Regia at Lazonby	Wilson (1976): Ferrar & Richardson (2003)	D4E
Hee Street	(Prescott 1887)	D4E
Castle Hewen boundary hedge	McGillivray (undated): Ferrar & Richardson (2003)	D2E
Barrock Fold boundary hedge	Ferrar & Richardson (2003)	D1E
Ferguson's "pre-Roman track"	Ferguson (1886)	D3W

To this day, between Carlisle and the Lake District there are a vast number of lanes, footpaths and field boundaries which, being inclined *Atan* 3/5 to the cardinal points, overlie the *limites* of cadaster B or the tracks within its *centuriae*. Some are listed in Table 4.4 where the bold type indicates that the chosen reference point stands on a *limes*. Two bold co-ordinates indicate a grid node.

TABLE 4.4: DISTANCES OF CERTAIN FEATURES FROM TETRANS B (EDEN-CALDEW CONFLUENCE)
K = kardo: D = decumanus:

Site	OS Grid Reference		Position relative to tetrans	
			Centuriae S	*Centuriae* E or W
1. Stripes	345.65	551.80	10.3	D4E
2. Sowerby Row	339.25	540.01	K19	D12W
3. Hee Street	348.00	547.90	K16.7	D4E
4. Southwaite	345.10	545.10	K18	1.5 W
5. High Northsceugh	352.84	548.10	K20	D10E
6. Calthwaite	346.75	540.31	K25	D3W
7. Blencowe	345.50	532.75	33.2	D10W
8. Dacre Church	345.90	526.55	K41	D14W
9. Stainton	348.40	527.90	41.2	D10W
10. Tirril	350.15	526.63	K44	8.8 W
11. Askham village	351.31	523.65	48.4	9.6 W
12. Gt. Strickland	353.35	522.75	K51	7.7 W
13. Morland	359.90	522.53	K56	DM

1. D4E is now marked by the road between Cumwhinton and Cotehill, through Stripes. It continued to the Hee Street and the *via regia* at Lazonby; see below.
2. The modern road at Sowerby Row runs close to this point and is aligned NNW.
3. D4E is marked by Hee Street.
4. K18 is now marked by the EW road through Southwaite.
5. K20S, represented by the Middlesceugh Hall-Barrow Mill line, coincides with a length of road connecting Northsceugh and High Northsceugh east of Eden. The road junction is about D10E. Thus, *Hutton Sceugh* and *Northsceugh* lie at each end of K20, between D30W and D10E, with *Middlesceugh* (D10W) in the middle.
6. Calthwaite village lies at the node of D3W and K25S, which is a *quintarius*. D3W is extant as a short stretch of apparently ancient road at Orchard House (OS 346.80 540.20). This was examined by George Richardson who was convinced of its antiquity, but

who could make no sense of its direction. The short length of road east of Ruckcroft (OS 353.30 544.30) also coincides with K25S between D7E and D8E, though there is little other evidence of *decumani* so far east.

7. Blencowe village stands at the junction of the Old Penrith-Troutbeck Roman road with D10W, which to the north is marked by the Middlesceugh Hall-Skelton road. South-east of Blencowe, D10W goes towards Pallet Hill, mentioned in the Inglewood Forest boundary amendment of Henry I. It might now be represented by the strip of plantation north of the house at Ennim and then by the lane passing east of Newbiggin over Hoghhouse Hill. This section of D10W may have been incorporated into the Inglewood Forest boundary road, as described above.

8. Dacre stands at a crossroads, if the road from Sparket be regarded as continuing by the footpath to Stainton, which it enters as the *Thorngate*. This alignment is along K41, while the NS road through Dacre follows D14W and north of the village, after the road bends eastwards, is marked by a hedge in line ahead.

9. Fairy Bead Lane, Stainton, aligns very closely to D10W.

10. The modern road through Tirril coincides with K44. The ditched *agger* along the boundary wall of Sockbridge Hall, identified as High Street by Collingwood [15] is very probably the remains of this *limes*.

11. Askham village lies in the centre of the *centuria* defined by D9W and D10W and K48 and K49. The field boundaries tend to be aligned on the *limites*, many quite obviously so. The village main street overlies the mid-centurial tracks and that going northwards continues into the next *centuria* as a field boundary. The lane to Celleron branches west from this line and soon turns on to D10W as far as K47 when it crosses to the next mid-centurial track, which it follows to K46, before bending to the west. In the middle of the second field north of Askham Hall, D9W can be seen as a roughly 12 feet wide *agger* running precisely on line for well over a hundred yards.

12. The main street of Great Strickland overlies K51.

13. The long foot path north-east of Little Strickland (OS 356.20 520.45 to 357.00 521.35) runs along K56 from D6W towards Morland, which lies very close to the K56 : DM node.

Figure 4.6 shows how the field boundaries and lanes in the vicinity of Low Braithwaite relate to the cadaster. These were laid out in about 1820 but their co-incidence with the *limites* is beyond question. Figure 4.7 shows how the modern field boundaries and lanes in the vicinity of Askham and Tirril relate to cadaster B in that area. The *limites* were identified by the spreadsheet outlined in Appendix 2.

Cadaster B seems to have extended laterally for at least 16 *centuriae* Sowerby Row to the Stripes - Hee Street - *via regia* line. The *sceugh* names hint that it may have extended to 40. The disposition of lanes and fields suggests the cadaster reached the vicinity of Shap, at K60. If the width were 20 centuriae, the total area was 1,200 *centuriae* or 48 *salti* (1 *saltus* = 25 centuriae) and is very plausible.[16] Of course, some of this land would have included fell and moorland which we should not expect to have interested the Roman authorities. Here we must remember that centuriation was not primarily about land use but ownership. The eastings and northings of the main lines of cadaster B are given in Appendix 11.

---

[15] Collingwood (1937)

[16] At Manchester there was a cadaster of two salti, one cadaster of one saltus and probably another larger one (Richardson 2004 a).

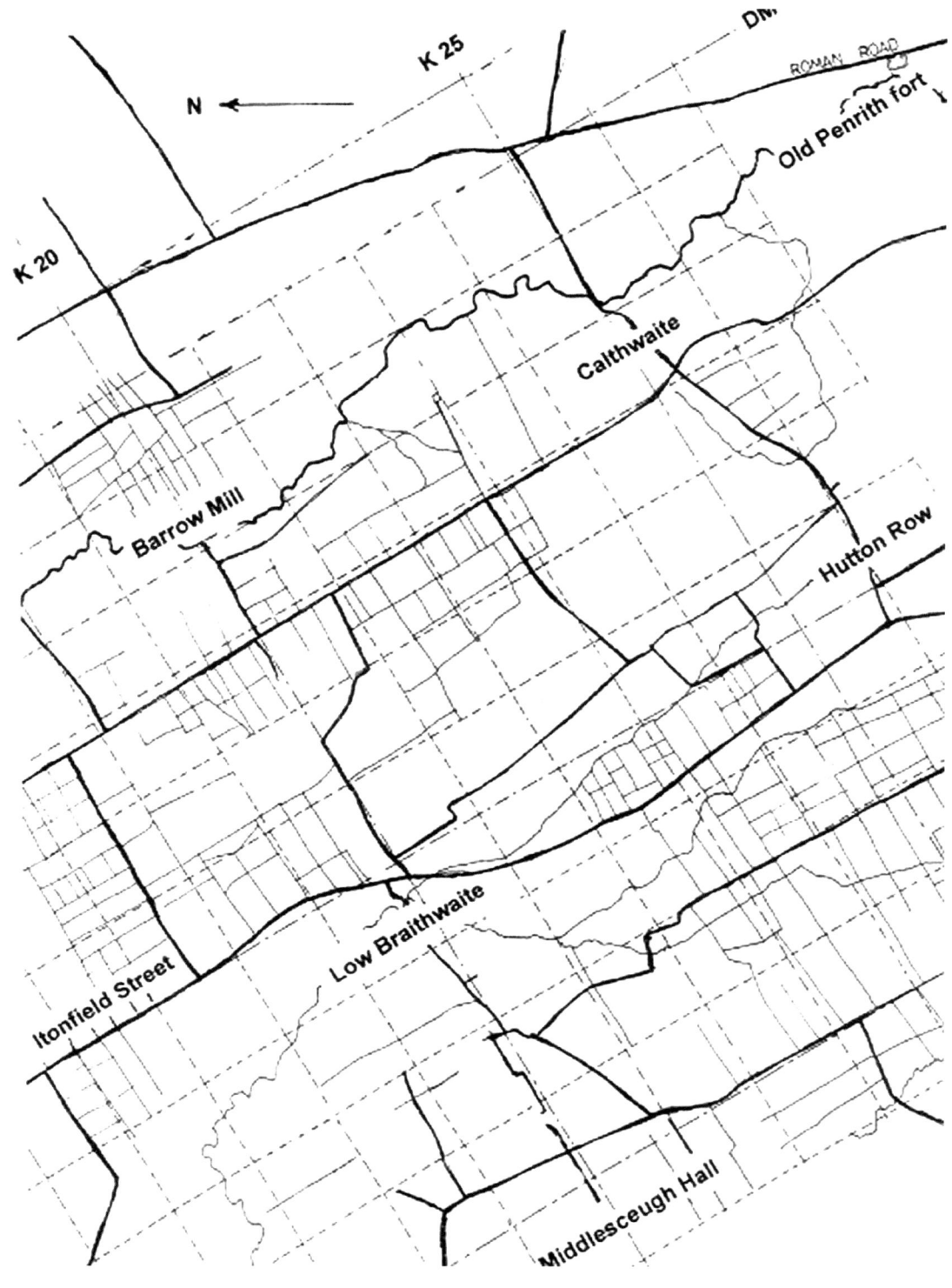

Figure 4.6:

Lanes and field boundaries in the vicinity of Low Braithwaite. Note how many run parallel to the *limites*. *Centuriae* of 20 *actus* indicated by dashed lines. (After Ferrar & Richardson 2003)

Figure 4.7

Lanes and field boundaries between Sockbridge and Helton. Askham is not labelled in order to reveal its field system. Its cross roads represent the intersection of the two mid-centurial tracks. (*Centuriae* of 20 *actus* indicated by dashed lines)

Centuriation at Old Penrith

The disposition of the fields and lanes near the Old Penrith fort suggested to both Michael Ferrar and me a possibly separate cadaster, since certain apparently significant lines did not quite fit with cadaster B.[17] For example, Plumpton crossroads were two centuriae south of the fort's via principalis, whilst the alignment of the EW arm of the crossroads could be projected some three miles eastwards to the Eden, where the last mile from Scatterbeck to the river, formed the perfectly straight Lazonby-Great Salkeld parish boundary. Further reflection, however, urges me to suspect that the modern lanes and field boundaries in the Plumpton area are probably more related to the main road.

---

[17] Ferrar & Richardson (2003)

Nonetheless, Low Street, suspected by Ferguson to be part of the pre-Roman track from Etterby to Penrith[18] seems to mark *limes* D3W.

The modern road (OS 354.05 538.00 to OS 353.37 540.59) runs somewhere near the mediaeval *via regia* which separated Lazonby demesne from Brownrigg. Wilson surmised that the *via regia* lay east of this modern road but careful reading of his quotes from the Holme Coultram charters reveals this was only because he guessed that a certain arable plot must have been in the town fields of Lazonby.[19] It precise location in this area therefore remains uncertain but I suspect it was along *limes* D4E. See above.

Aiktongate

The elucidation of cadaster A raised questions about the significance of Newbiggin Road which, between Durdar and Newbiggin Hall, coincides with K7S (A). This road turns out to be part of a route that once connected the crossing of the Caldew at Hawksdale, Dalston, to Hayton and thence to Hadrian's Wall near Lanercost Bridge. As such, it explains the existence of these two otherwise oddly sited ancient river crossings. See Figure 4.8 which shows the main alignments in relation to the cadasters.

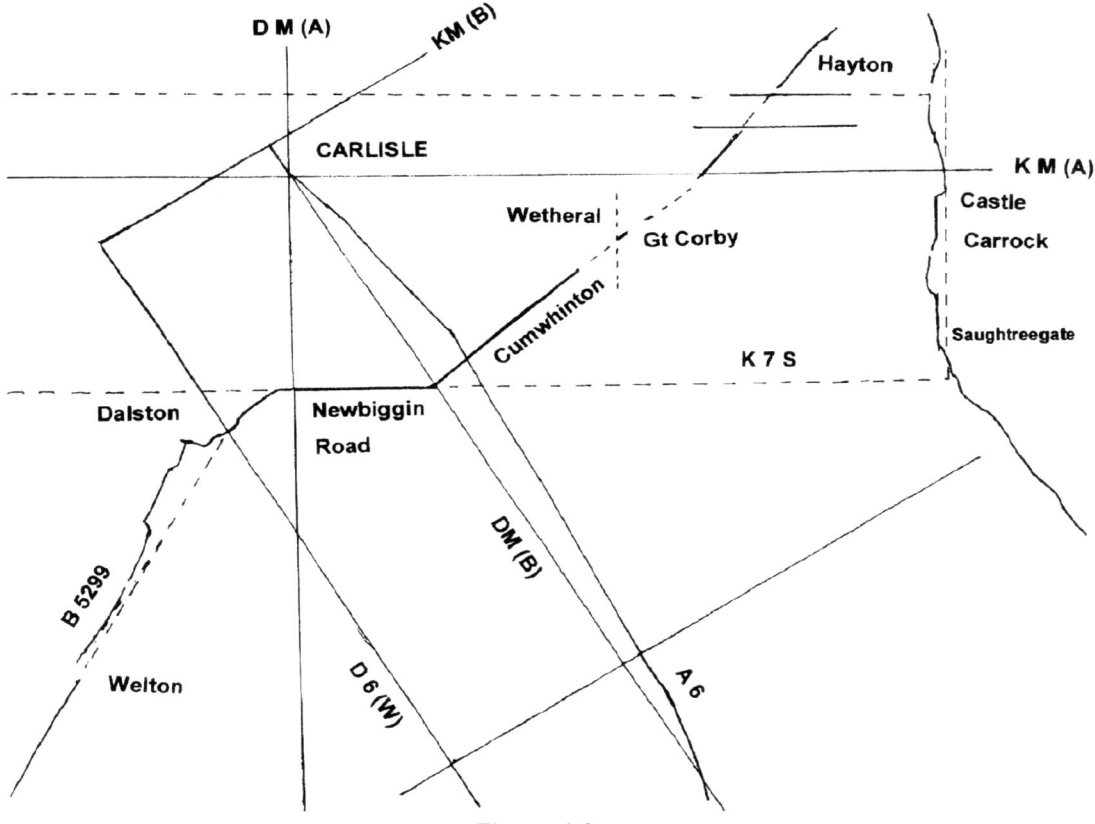

Figure 4.8
Aiktongate in relation to cadasters A and B. (Scale: tetrans A to Newbiggin road = seven centuriae)

The alignments, going east from Dalston, are as follows:

Alignment 1 (2.2 miles): A line from Hawksdale bridge (OS 337.00 549.15) to the west end of Newbiggin Road at a point just east of the lane to Park Fauld (OS 339.75 550.95)

---

[18] Ferguson (1886)
[19] Wilson (1976)

with *limes* K7 (B). The modern road between those points first meanders about the line but then coincides with it from just east of Green Lane, [D6W (B)]. Just east of Park Fauld, half a mile west of Durdar, the modern road turns onto the second alignment.

Alignment 2 (2.3 miles): The road now becomes Newbiggin Road and runs due east to Newbiggin Hall (OS 343.2 551.00). It is virtually coincident with K7S (A) though the modern carriageway crosses it at a very shallow angle.

Alignment 3 (4.6 miles): Close by Newbiggin Hall, the shift to alignment 3 (*Atan* 3/4 N of E) is along the pre-motorway road that crossed the river Petteril and the Carlisle-Brougham Roman road (A6) at Golden Fleece. The line is then shadowed by the modern road through Cumwhinton to Wetheral Abbey. Here alignment 3 crosses the Eden at an ancient ford and continues along Great Corby's main street, which is clearly an ancient hollow-way, to a short disused lane and footpath going to a hamlet (OS 348.50 555.22) significantly named Broadwath (broad ford) in 1285.[20]

Alignment 4 (7.0 miles): The line then shifts (Atan 6/5 N of E) along the modern road towards Hayton village, passing just east of Toppin Castle. There is a half-mile gap across the fields south of Hayton, beyond which the line coincides with the modern road from Hayton to Low Gelt Bridge. Thereafter alignment 4 is shadowed by the modern A 69 road to Brampton, and then may be projected through Brampton onto the lane going to Great Easby and passing about half a mile east of Cotehill Farm. The alignment reaches the river Irthing below Lanercost Bridge (OS 354.90 563.40) just west of the Stanegate fort at Boothby.

A short distance north of here, an ancient drove road known as *Hayton Gate* crossed the Wall at Tower 53b.[21] This would be an obvious name for a road heading for Hayton along the line just described, but it appears that *Hayton* Gate was formerly *Aikton* Gate, (Aiktongate, 1589: Aytongate, 1603: Aicktongate, 1620) though there was no such place in the area to justify the name. [22] [23] Discussing this, the place-name experts, not unreasonably, discounted the notion that it might have connected with Aikton, near Wigton. However, it seems possible that it did go towards that place along the alignments given above. West of Durdar a track along K7S (A) would have continued to Aikton with the A 596 road at Low Whinnow, on northing OS 551.00, perhaps now representing it. For the sake of simplicity, though with some licence, I shall now refer to the whole putative route as *Aiktongate*.

Almost all the 15 Roman miles from Hawksdale Bridge to Low Gelt Bridge coincides with, or is shadowed by, modern road. The only gap is the half mile between Toppin Castle and Hayton village. The whole route is shown on Hodgkinson and Donald's map (*circa* 1775) where the central part of Newbiggin Road is missing though, very significantly, each extremity is marked. The same map shows the road from Great Corby to Broadwath following what is now the footpath. Another map of 1704 indicates that between the Hayton parish boundary and How Street, it had already formed a base line for enclosures.[24]

This undoubtedly very old route neatly fits the provincial Roman survey grid. See Table 4.5 which shows how its alignments shift at NS *centuria* intersections relative to Wall Knowe. But there are few other clues that hint at the road's Roman origin, apart from its proximity

---

[20] Armstrong et al (undated, 161)

[21] Bruce (1863, 180)

[22] Armstrong et al (undated, 71)

[23] At Haytongate Farm (OS 356.40 564.60) a newly made field lane (OS 356.40 564.60) overlies an older strip of cobbling coming down through the field from the gap in the Wall and pointing to Lanercost bridge; information from Mrs Foster of Abbey Farm, Lanercost.

[24] Graham (1907)

to the Boothby fort. In a field on Wetheral Abbey farm (OS 346.15 553.75) there is a ditched and embanked rectangular enclosure whose proportions suggest a Roman fortlet.[25] Its name, "Harbour" Wood, may well be significant - see above. There was also a Roman temporary camp by the Golden Fleece.[26] Within a house at Crossroads House, Brisco, there a deep, and reputedly Roman, well. However, the route would have afforded a good lateral connection from south-west of Carlisle to the mid-Wall and may have linked with Caldbeck; a matter to be discussed in Part 5.

TABLE 4.5: ALIGNMENT NODES ON AIKTONGATE IN RELATION TO WALL KNOWE

	OS grid references		EW		NS	
From Wall Knowe	340.67	557.40	actus	cents	actus	cents
1. Newbiggin Rd West	339.75	550.95	26 W	1.3 W	180 S	9.0 S
2. Newbiggin Rd East	343.15	551.00	77 E	3.5 E	179 S	8.9 S
3. Broadwath	348.50	555.22	220 E	11.0 E	60 S	3.0 S

Sequence of development

The relationship of "Aiktongate" to both cadasters suggests a possible developmental sequence. Newbiggin Road, though not a *quintarius*, marks *limes* K7S (A). However, beginning at Hawksdale Bridge, it first coincides with K7 (B). This suggests that it was laid down after both cadasters were established. The Brougham - Carlisle road line does not coincide with the *limites* of cadaster B, (save at High Hesket) and the pottery evidence from the Scalesceugh tilery suggests the road was early Flavian.[27] But cadaster B fits-in with Hadrian's Wall and is unlikely to be earlier. Therefore the suggested sequence is:

1. Brougham-Carlisle road completed (Flavian, *circa* AD 75).
2. Cadaster A set out (AD 75-120).
3. Hadrian's Wall, Aiktongate and cadaster B (after AD 120).

Cadaster A probably extended for over 20 miles from Kirkbride to Castle Carrock. Originally, it may well have extended 10 *centuriae* NS, giving an area of at least 440 *centuriae*. But there is no evidence of its *kardines* close to the Wall, nor immediately south of Carlisle, where the roads tend to fan out from the city towards the *decumani* of cadaster B; that is to Dalston, Durdar, Brisco and Cotehill. It looks as if the north-central part of cadaster A was obliterated by the Wall system, while cadaster B was made to overlie its central portion, but leaving cadaster A *limites* more or less intact east of the Eden and west of the Carlisle - Papcastle road. There are a few clues suggesting cadaster B *decumani* east of the Eden, most noticeably the Warwick Bridge - Heads Nook road which appears to straddle D12E (B). Overlapping cadasters were quite common.[28]

---

[25] The site was reported to the Cumbria County Council Sites and Monuments Record Dept. Photographs are lodged at Tullie House. It is shown clearly marked on the 1866 six inch OS map.
[26] Welfare & Swan (1995, 38)
[27] Richardson (1973, 82)
[28] Bradford (1957, 163)

Fate of the cadasters

During the Roman period the centuriated land was probably fully exploited and doubtless the metalled roads were repaired and the tracks kept clean. But the collapse of the imperial government and the drift to subsistence farming would have seen a neglect of this infrastructure. Unmanaged woodland would soon revert to "waste". Yet the evidence suggests that sufficient lengths of track and some of the less substantial boundaries survived through the middle Ages. Indeed, if the alignments of the vast number of modern field boundaries and footpaths are regarded as significant, then a great many intra-centurial divisions survived. The boundary hedges at Hesket noted by Bowey in 1715 have gone, but many other *limites* were undoubtedly incorporated into enclosures made between the 13th and 19th centuries. During this process, where old lanes were not utilised, new ones were often laid down alongside, or in the general vicinity. Anyone who takes the trouble of drawing the proposed *limites* on the OS map cannot fail to be astonished by the vast number of field boundaries, lanes and footpaths that lie parallel to them. It is also clear that a great many villages of mediaeval origin lie very close to the *limites*, hinting that later settlers found the tracks convenient. The relative paucity of Roman artefacts within the cadasters is of no significance whatever. The population was probably never high and the area was given over to agriculture and forestry.

If this exposition is accepted, our perception of the landscape in the middle Ages is radically changed, for then the whole countryside bore witness to the ancient civilisation as eloquently as did the crumbled streets in the vicinity of the ruined forts. The people of those days would have been very aware that this district was formerly governed by a power and intelligence that dwarfed their own, and it is not surprising that their piecemeal enclosures often followed more ancient boundaries.

Future Work

I referred above to the several mediaeval subdivisions of the Inglewood Forest known as *serjeanties*. It would be useful if some mediaeval scholar would describe these holdings, particularly their boundaries. I strongly suspect that many would coincide with the *limites* of cadaster B.

It would be of great interest to locate and excavate the site of Mabil Cross. There may be evidence of Roman activity in the form of votive offerings buried by the *agrimensores*. Furthermore, it is relevant to know when and why this monument was destroyed; the only plausible historic contexts for such desecration would be the Reformation and the Civil War, but it is not easy to see why iconoclasts should have singled out this remote site for destruction.

There remains the great task of describing the *limites* in detail with reference to the modern landscape and cartographical features. This will shed more light on the subject and perhaps throw light on the early history of particular parishes. To help with this work, the spreadsheets described in Appendices 1 and 2 will be useful, but for those without recourse to the computer, I have set out the OS grid references of main 5-*centuria* nodes of both cadasters in Appendices 9 and 9.

***

---

[29] Summerson (1991, 60)

PART FIVE

EVIDENCE OF OTHER ROMAN ROADS AND CADASTERS

Roads at Caldbeck

The modern map shows that the road going west from Durdar, mentioned above as part of *Aiktongate*, after bending onto *limes* K7 (B), follows its mean line to Hawksdale Bridge where it meets the Dalston-Caldbeck road (B 5299). This road comprises two more or less parallel alignments separated by an 'S' bend at Welton, and was shown on Hodkinson and Donald's map. The inclination of the southern section, between Welton and Warnell Fell at the lane to Rylands Farm, is *Atan* 3/5 E of N; see Table 5.1. In the light of what we now know of Roman road alignments, this is surely significant. When this line is projected north of Welton, it impinges on the Aiktongate at Green Lane, Pow Bank, so it looks as if a Roman road came over Warnell Fell from Caldbeck and at Welton turned towards Hawksdale Bridge and perhaps Carlisle.

TABLE 5.1: ROAD (B5299) ALIGNMENT BETWEEN WARNELL FELL AND WELTON

	OS reference		Centuriae from Wall Knowe		Distance	Atan
			W	S	miles	
Rylands Lane	333.25	540.90	10.5	23.2		
Welton	335.25	544.25	7.6	18.5	2.64	0.60 (3/5)

South of Welton the B 5299 road rises up to the top of Warnell Fell and turns west through a right-angle but the main alignment continues along the lane to Rylands Farm. Beside this lane are numerous grassed-over stone pits, regarded by some as good indicators of a Roman road. From the farm a footpath continues the line through a field on the southern slope of Warnell Fell as an un-kerbed metalled strip that curves westwards at the bottom of the field. The continuing line is then marked by a series of ditches whose position suggests they may once have served as a boundary rather than as drains, because they tend to run above the surrounding ground. It is possible to suggest, but impossible to prove, that these were once the marginal ditches of an ancient road. The ditch line goes down to the field north of Caldbeck church, pointing to the old bridge over the beck. There are no obvious signs of a road continuing on this line south of Caldbeck church, but the projected line soon meets the *Street* from Hesket Newmarket, "the old King's road" to the river Ellen, mentioned in Part Two. It seems highly likely that a Roman road from the southern part of the coastal defence system went north-eastwards through Caldbeck to connect, via Welton and the Aiktongate, with the middle part of the Wall. Further study is needed. See Figure 5.1.

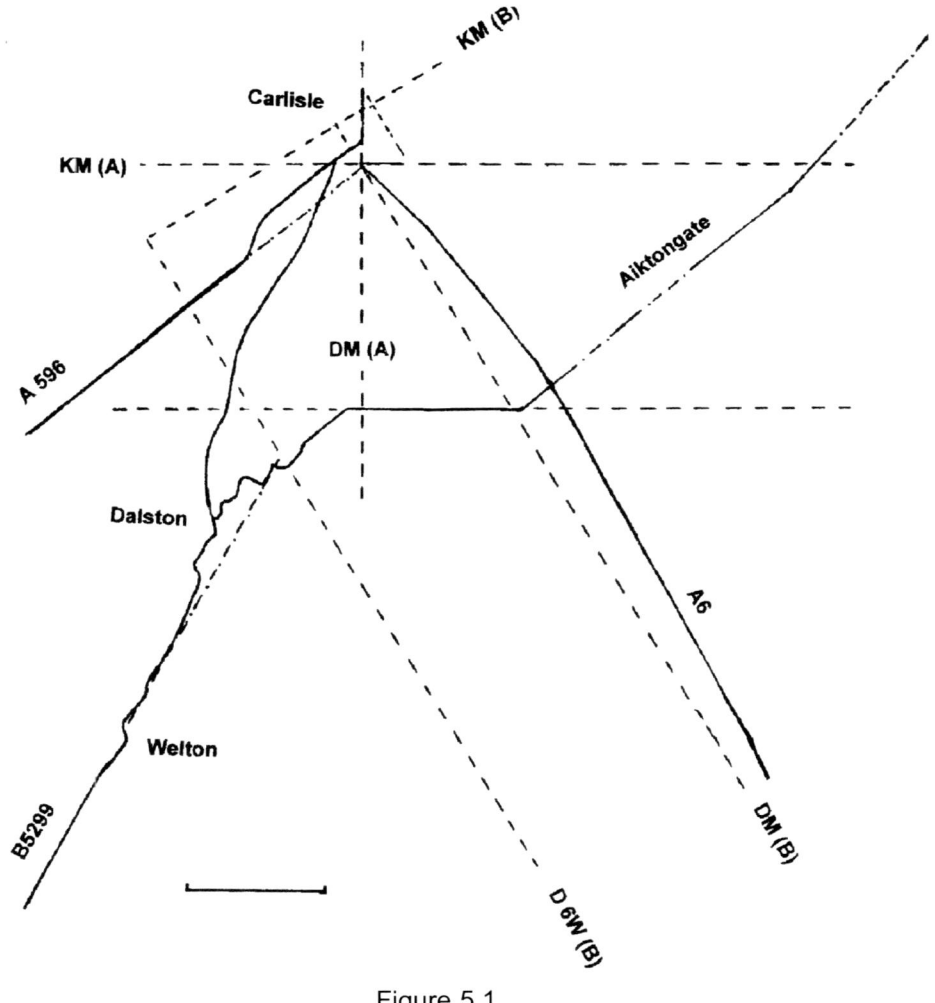

Figure 5.1

Warnell - Dalston road in relation to cadasters A and B : Scale = 80 actus

Corbridgegate

There is good literary evidence of a Roman road connecting Corbridge with Penrith. It comes from references to the *Corbriggate* at Alston in the 12th, 13th and 14th centuries, and one from the 15th century which specifically refers to its going to Penrith. North east of Alston, a straight two-mile alignment of modern road, farm lane and track probably marks its course. From OS 372.50 549.00 on the A686, a farm lane runs to Moscow Farm and is continued by a field boundary and track which rejoins the A686 at OS 373.90 550.80. From thence to the county boundary a reduced *agger* accompanies the road just over the wall on the west. From the county boundary the modern road enters open moorland and the heather covered *agger* on its western side becomes very substantial; five metres wide with marginal ditches. At OS 374.75 552.00, the modern road swings east but the line of the *agger* is maintained, with a slight shift of alignment, as a metalled track across the moor to the modern road at OS 375.00 555.00. The main part of this line between Whitehouse and Hartside Cross inclines *Atan* 3/4 E of N. See Table 5.2. The fact that the name *Corbriggate*, rather than *Hexhamgate*, clung to a road in Alston strongly hints that it predated the foundation of Hexham Abbey and was associated with the Roman town.

---

[2] Richardson (2002)
[3] Armstrong et al, (undated, 151)

TABLE 5.2: ALIGNMENTS RELATED TO THE CORBRIDGEGATE

	OS reference		Centuriae from Wall Knowe		Distance	Atan
			E	S	miles	
Whitehouse	372.50	549.00	44.8	11.8		
Gate at OS ref	374.75	552.00	48.0	7.5	2.54	0.75 (3/4)
Whitley Castle	369.50	548.80	40.6	12.0		
Brougham	353.45	528.95	18.0	40.0	17.26	0.8 (4/5)
Hartside	364.8	541.75	34.0	22.0		
Brougham	353.45	528.95	18.0	40.0	11.57	0.9 (9/10)

The Corbridgegate probably went to Brougham and part of its course is probably marked by the modern road (A686) from Alston to Hartside Cross (OS 364.80 541.75). From there the modern road descends along the western face of Fiend's Fell, but the older line, marked on the OS map and still traceable on the ground, passed south of the modern café and went down to Two Top Bridge (OS 362.85 541.10). It may have then continued by an old, sunken way to Gamblesby, shown on old maps, but it is more likely to have coincided more or less with the modern road to Langwathby, crossing the Eden by the old ford above the modern bridge (OS 356.95 533.40). It would then have continued by Edenhall's main street to regain the A 686 road before Carleton, where it would join the road from Carlisle as it descended to Brougham. A line from Hartside Cross to Brougham inclines *Atan* 0.9 (9/10) S of W. At the same time, a line from Whitley Castle fort to Brougham is inclined *Atan* 0.8 (4/5) S of W. See Table 5.2 which sets out the relationships of the main alignments of the Corbridgegate. This appears to be another example of a geometric road design line being modified to take account of the local topography.

Hartside Cross to Renwick

From the *Corbridgegate* at Hartside Cross, a road once branched north westwards to Renwick [3]. See Figure 5.2. It is still very evident, cutting through the hair-pin bend on the modern road just below Hartside summit. This section appears quite modern and obviously existed before the hair-pen bend was made, but its original line is continued through a gate into open moorland. The first 80 metres comprise a roughly metalled track which then turns westward and runs for some 800 metres straight down the fellside. Throughout its length are remnants of a stout, cobbled, four metre-wide *agger* running between marginal ditches, marked by rushes and running water. The causeway is perfectly straight and is accompanied by a narrower, and apparently later, metalled track, hopping from side to side. There is nothing certainly Roman about this section but where the gradient becomes steeper (OS 363.93 542.18) there is a 20-metre length of *agger*, five metres wide within marginal ditches; a typical Roman causeway. Then at OS 363.83 542.20 another section of *agger* continues the alignment, but now a two metre-wide hollow way, devoid of metalling, appears on the north and sweeps out in a 40-metre loop, regaining the original line 60 metres further down. This hollow way then loops to the south and regains the straight alignment as a 12 feet deep trench at OS 363.73 542.22. The looping hollow way and straight *agger* between them make a dollar

---

[3]Richardson (2004 b)

sign, thus $. Throughout this section, the *agger*, cambered and in places well-metalled, marks the main alignment. It is very clear that we have an original, straight road that was used by travellers who left it, where it became too steep, to create a hollow way that zig-zagged down the hillside. This zig-zag is deeply scoured and very obviously scars the fell-side when viewed from the west. At OS 363.63 542.23, is the best preserved portion of *agger* running for 25 metres between marginal ditches. Sixty metres further on, the road line meets a beck.

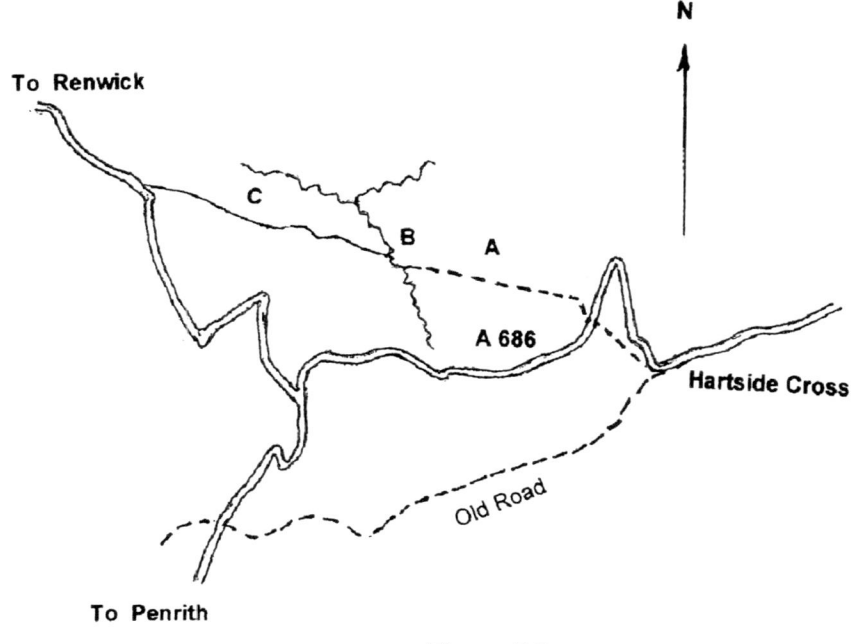

Figure 5.2
Roads from Hartside Cross: A = ditched agger, B = Ricker Gill bridge, C = modern track

This is the Ricker Gill, running northwards in a ravine which the road, now a mere stony path, crosses by a stout stone bridge, perhaps better described as a stone-faced embankment pierced by a culvert. The way across the bridge is now about two metres wide, the north side having collapsed into the ravine. It is 20 metres from one side to the other and the original abutments on the north side show it was once eight metres wide. On the south there is a reduced parapet whose top is four metres above the beck. The culvert is 1.8 metres wide and about one metre high. It has a keystone arch with eight large stones on either side. The stonework is high quality and laid in straight courses with three zones which become cruder nearer the top; five courses from the ground to the level of the arch keystone: four courses of bigger stones for about two metres: a third course (three rows) of very large stones up to the top. It seems as if at least two phases are represented; an earlier characterised by fine masonry and a later with much larger, cruder stone work.

West of the beck, the causeway comprises about 60 metres of cobbled way which leads onto a firm, level and apparently modern road, hugging the contour for about quarter of a mile towards Selah. However, the original line can be seen from the hill on the east above the bridge vanishing into the heather from where it cannot be traced further. The apparently modern road goes to a ruined cottage at OS 363.00 542.39. From there the way is a modern farm road which reaches the public highway at OS 362.40 542.55, *en route* to Haresceugh and the bridge over the Raven Beck. Appleby Street crossed this beck about 100 yards lower down by a now lost bridge whose northern abutment remains *in situ* and alongside which are the remains of a ditched *agger* [4]. The mean line of the road between Hartside Cross and Raven Bridge is *Atan* 3/10 N of W. See Table 5.3.

TABLE 5.3: MEAN ROAD ALIGNMENT BETWEEN HARTSIDE CROSS AND RAVEN BRIDGE

	OS reference		Centuriae from Wall Knowe		Distance	Atan
			W	S	miles	
Hartside Cross	364.80	541.75	34.0	22.0		
Raven Bridge	360.10	543.15	27.4	20.0	3.32	0.30 (3/10) N of W

The historic and geographic contexts of the bridge over the Ricker Gill and the *agger* and ditched causeway approaching it from the east, strongly suggest a Roman origin. This road connected two other Roman roads along an original and well-engineered line that was avoided by later traffic whose passage gave rise to the hollow way at the steepest part. Pack horsemen crossing the open country from Hartside to Renwick would not have taken this route had it not already existed because it crosses the Ricker Gill at a precipitous ravine that would more sensibly have been avoided by going a little to the north. This road and bridge was the work of engineers for whom line was more important than topographical convenience and for whom the ravine was a minor obstacle. Indeed, the whole feature affords a unique juxtaposition of Roman, mediaeval and modern causeways upon a single short length of road.

Appleby Street - Thief Street

After realising that Roman roads were frequently designed by connecting nodes on a map grid, I determined the angle of alignment of Appleby Street, the 30-mile Roman road along the Eastern Fells, apparently connecting Castlesteads Wall fort with the Brougham-Brough road (A66) at Castrigg [5]. The mean course was Atan 2/5 W of N. From Castrigg to the Raven Beck, Appleby Street followed this mean alignment but at the Raven Beck the line shifted to *Atan* 7/10 W of N and is now marked by the B6413 road as far as Saughtreegate (OS 354.15 551.64). This point is a node of cadaster A (D 20E: K6S). Here, the B 6413 road turns onto Appleby Street's third alignment, going northwards along *limes* D20E towards its junction with Thief Street. See Table 5.4 and Figure 5.3

Graham (1907) reported that Thief Street, SSE of Low Gelt Bridge, was used by rievers *en route* to Appleby. It cut obliquely across the north-east corner of cadaster A, but there is no extant evidence south of Two Top, where the traceable *agger* ends at the railway (OS 352.85 557.10) [6] [7]. The mean line between Low Gelt Bridge and Two Top is inclined *Atan* 2/5 W of N. See Table 5.5. When this line is continued, it goes to a point about OS 354.15 553.80, on the Saughtreegate-Brampton road between Long Dyke and Long Dyke Farm. This is at cadaster A node D20E : K 3S. This was confirmed trigonometrically by the spreadsheet given at Appendix 1. North of the river Gelt, there is no obvious evidence of Thief Street

---

[4] Mr Richard Brockington and I sectioned the agger remains at this point and identified a marginal ditch. The relevant drawings are lodged at Tullie House, Carlisle.

[5] Richardson (1984)

[6] Graham (1907)

[7] Richardson (2002)

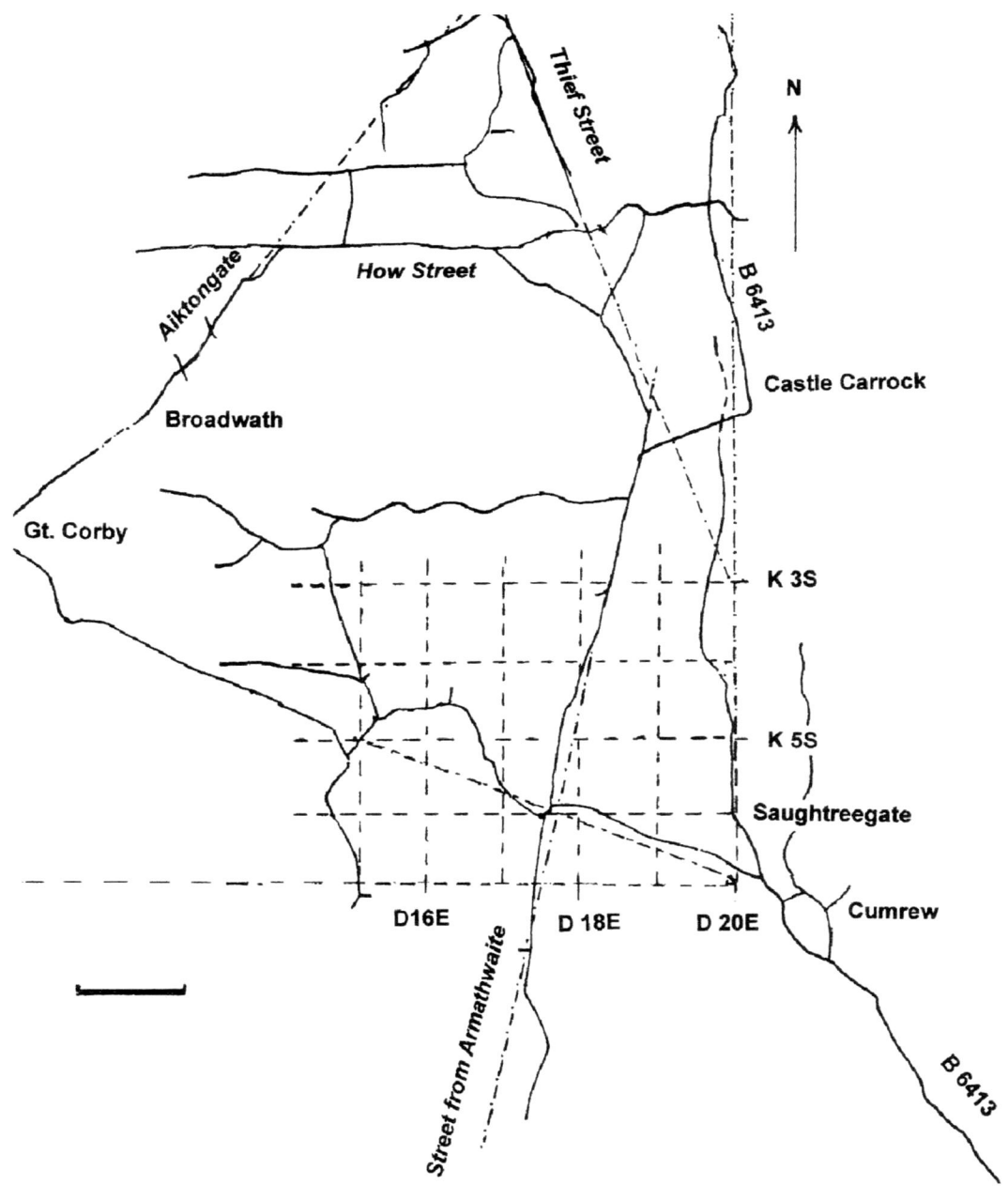

Figure 5.3

Thief Street - Appleby Street (B6413) in relation to cadaster A and Thief Street: The Roman road from Renwick probably reached the south-east corner of the cadaster south of Saughtreegate: Scale = 1 km

TABLE 5.4: ALIGNMENTS OF APPLEBY STREET

	OS reference		Centuriae from Wall Knowe		Distance	Atan
			E	NS	miles	
Main alignment						
Castlesteads	351.50	563.50	15.3	8.7 N		
Castrigg	368.15	521.55	38.7	50.4 S	30.5	0.40 (2/5)
Alignment 1.						
Raven Beck	360.05	543.00	27.3	20.2 S		
Castrigg	368.15	521.55	38.7	50.4 S	15.5	0.38 (2/5)
Alignment 2.						
Saughtreegate	354.15	551.64	19.0	8.0 S		
Raven Beck	360.05	543.00	27.3	20.2 S	7.09	0.69 (7/10)
Alignment 3.						
Thief Street S end	354.15	553.80	16.0	5.0 S		
Saughtreegate	354.15	551.64	19.0	8.0 S	1.46	-

The B6413 road north of Appleby Street's junction with Thief Street, near Long Dyke, continues to mark *limes* D20E (A).* At Castle Carrock, it makes a right-angled bend, but the main alignment continues to the river Gelt by a lane west of, and parallel to, the village main street. North of the river, the *limes* is represented again by the B6413 towards Brampton, though the coincidence is not precise, no doubt due to the attrition, repair and minor re-alignments of centuries.

TABLE 5.5: ALIGNMENT OF THIEF STREET

	OS reference		Centuriae from Wall Knowe		Distance	Atan
			E	S	miles	
Low Gelt Br.	352.00	559.15	16.0	2.5		
Two Top	352.90	557.00	17.2	0.5	1.58	0.4 (2/5) W of N

Thus Appleby Street-Thief Street by passed Brampton because before the Middle Ages that place had no importance. Later, travellers going southwards from Brampton followed the extant *quintarius*, D20E (A), to the Appleby Street-Thief Street junction. A similar development seems to have happened at Ashton under Lyne, Lancashire, where the Manchester-Melandra Roman road passed south of a town which did not exist, or was of no importance, in the Roman period. But the Roman road was the very line that Ashton was "under" [8].

---

* The name, Long Dyke, might refer to a bank marking the limes.

[8] Richardson (2004 a)

Saughtreegate-Great Corby-Carlisle

Just south of Saughtreegate, a side road branches westwards and a discontinuous, straight line of roads and tracks, going via Carlattan and Cumwhitton to Great Corby, suggests the junction was once linked to Carlisle. It inclines *Atan* 2/5 N of W and would have cut through the corners of the *centuriae* of cadaster A at every five west to two north; a type of arrangement seen in Roman cadasters elsewhere [9]. It may well have continued west of the Eden by the road that is now Wetheral Plains and thus joined the main road east from Carlisle. See Table 5.6 and Figure 5.3. This line also intrigued George Richardson but it lacked the conventional clues to a Roman origin.

TABLE 5.6: SOME PUTATIVE ROMAN ROAD LINES IN THE EDEN VALLEY

	OS reference		Centuriae from Wall Knowe		Distance	Atan
			E	NS	miles	
Saughtreegate (J)	354.20	551.00	19.1	9.0		
Gt. Corby	347.05	553.85	9.0	4.9	5.21	0.4 (2/5) N of W
The Street *						
Armathwaite	351.45	546.60	15.2	15.1		
Ringate (south)	353.20	555.40	17.7	2.7	6.1	0.20 (1/5) E of N

* Beginning of the second straight alignment east of the river as far as the junction south of Ringate.

The Street from Armathwaite

The 18th century map, showing Thief Street connecting with the *Street* from Armathwaite, does not allow that road to be identified with certainty[10]. However it is unlikely to have followed any other line than the modern road between Hornsbygate and Tarn Lodge. It would cross the southwest corner of cadaster A to join Thief Street-Appleby Street, on Castle Carrock Common, as the old map showed. Its very existence would also suggest a Roman crossing of the Eden at Armathwaite. See Table 5.6 and Figure 5.3.

Renwick-Armathwaite

A straight line drawn on the map from Hartside to Armathwaite bridge is shadowed closely by the almost certain Roman road across the Ricker Gill, via Haresceugh, to Renwick, and then by a continuous and discontinuous series of lanes through Ainstable to Armathwaite. This is another plausible Roman line, though at present there is no confirmatory evidence. See Table 5.5 and Figure 5.4.

---

[9] Richardson (2004 a)

[10] Anon (undated)

Roman road network in the middle and lower Eden valley

Figure 5.4 shows the putative Roman road network in the lower Eden valley as outlined above. This reconstruction fits together well and is quite plausible. The separate pieces of evidence were identified from independent clues, so there is no circular argument involved. It would appear that Appleby Street was Hadrianic, since its design line included Castlesteads, but its third alignment made use of cadaster A which therefore predated it, as already suggested.

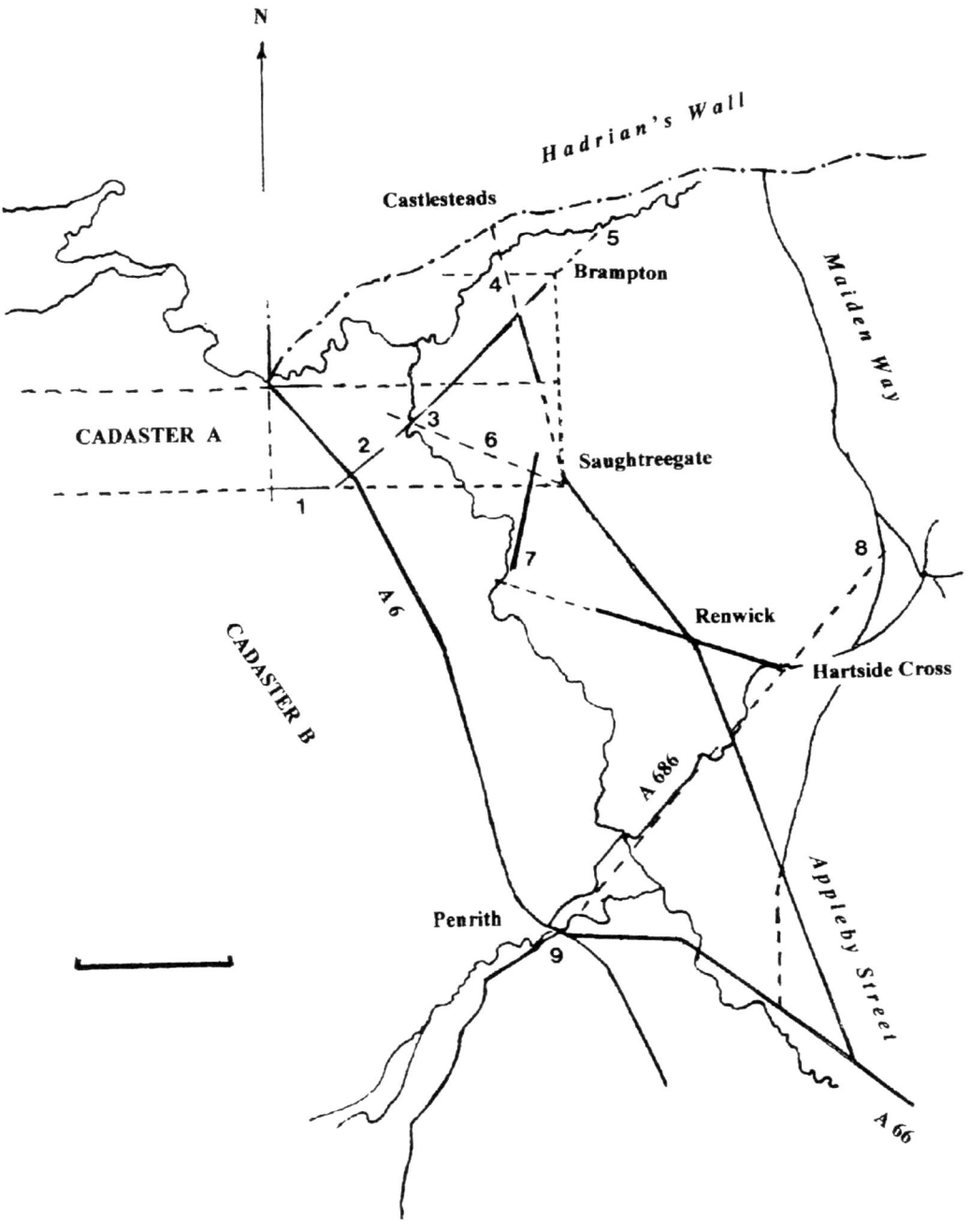

Figure 5.4

Roman road lines in the Eden valley: (1) Newbiggin Rd : (2) Cumwhinton : (3) Gt. Corby : (4) Thief Street : (5) Lanercost: (6) Cumwhitton: (7) The Street from Armathwaite to Castle Carrock Common: (8) Whitley Castle : (9) Brougham: Scale 5km

A possible cadaster at Kirkby Thore

The disposition of certain modern roads in the vicinity of the fort at Kirkby Thore hints at another cadaster aligned on the Brougham-Stainmore Roman road. Figure 5.5 illustrates this. Such an arrangement is to be expected, though more work is needed.

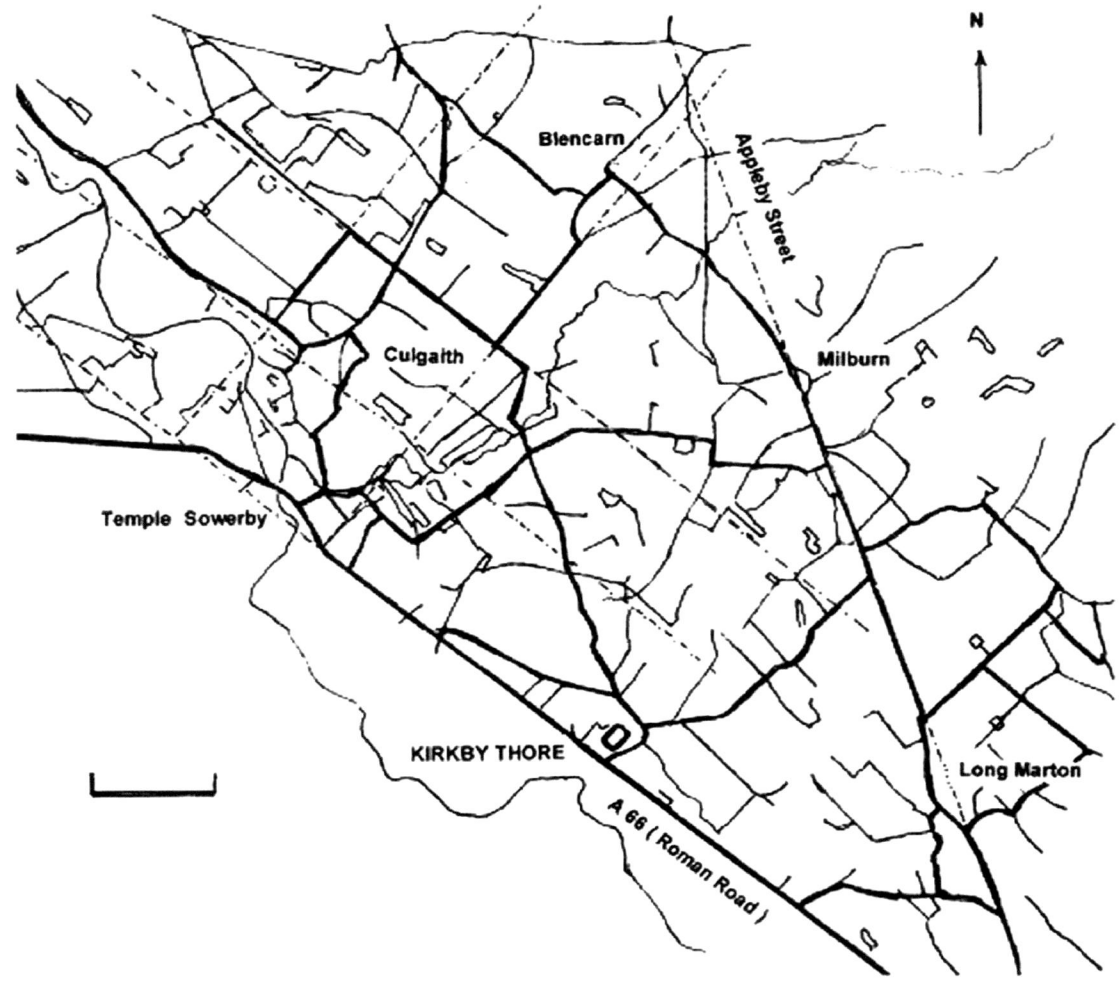

Figure 5.5
Possible cadaster near Kirkby Thore: Scale = 1 km

A possible cadaster in the Lune valley

South of the Low Borrowbridge fort, the main Roman road runs due south on the east side of the river Lune. South of Middleton and west of the river, two roads run parallel to it at about one *centuria* interval. One was known as the *Gallowgate* which clearly indicates an ancient route to Scotland, but again this makes no sense as a major road duplicating the known Roman road running up the valley. The Gallowgate and its partner may represent the *limites* of another cadaster and warrant further attention.

The East Cumberland landscape after Hadrian

The evidence reviewed in this book suggests that even before the Hadrianic frontier was established, Carlisle was the centre of a cadaster that extended from the coast to the Gelt. After Hadrian the frontier hinterland was further developed and exploited for crops, pasture, hay, livestock and timber on a scale probably not seen again until the 18th century. The road network was developed to enable rapid transit of troops and goods along and across the Eden valley and to enhance communication between the south-western coast and the mid-Wall.

The modern lanes and field boundaries between Carlisle and Shap still suggest a landscape that was geometrically ordered, yet conformed to the general land relief. It must have supported a population which supplied the needs of the great frontier market. Some land may have been held by contractors and the agents of wealthy businessmen who operated through freedmen and slaves, but much probably went to veteran freeholders. Almost certainly some land was returned to the natives, the presence of whose huts in no way precludes the survey having taken place. It is a reasonable guess that this landscape, had it been possible to view it from the air, would have appeared as a pleasant, dappled patchwork of fields and woods regularly laid out in strips or squares.

***

APPENDICES

Appendix 1: Formulae for calculating the OS co-ordinates of nodes on an angled grid

The spreadsheet gives the OS co-ordinates of nodes of a grid from a central datum point, the distances being in *actus*. See Figure A1.

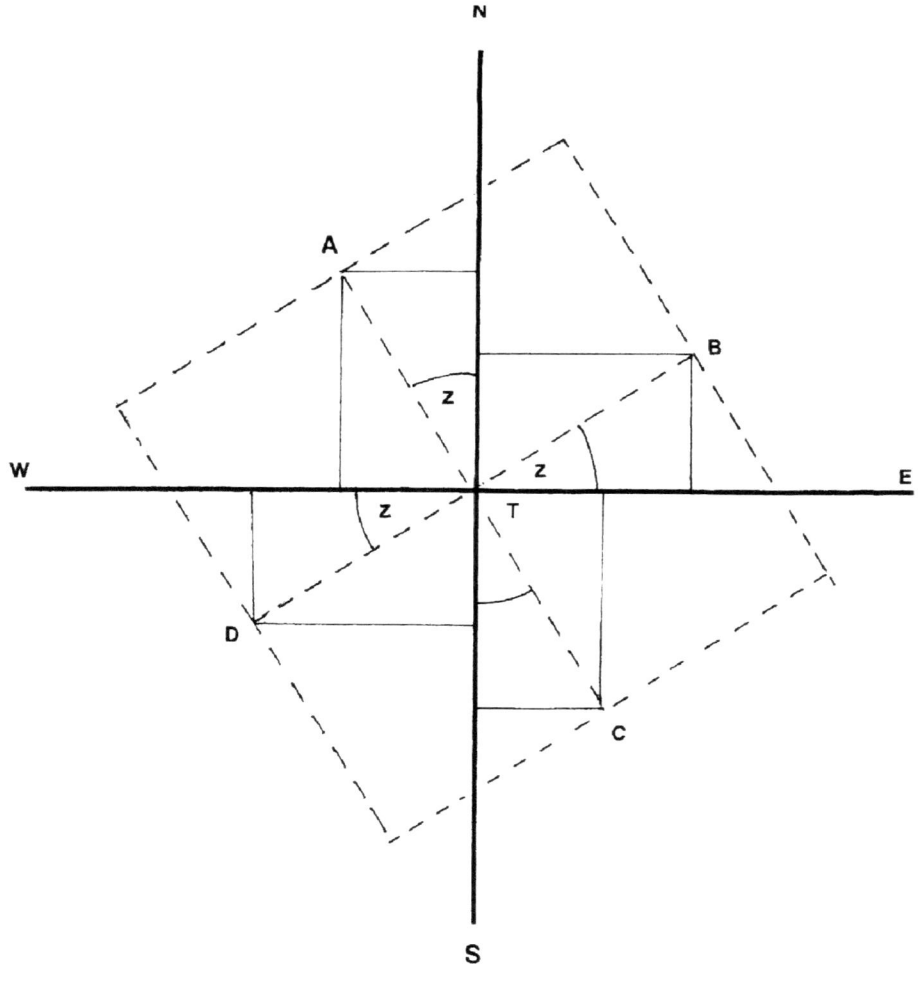

Figure A1

To convert distances in km. to Roman measure, multiply by 1000 and again by 39.36; then divide by 11.65 to give Roman feet. To change this to Roman miles, divide by 5000. To change feet to *actus*, divide by 120. To change *actus to centuriae* divide by 20.

A northing at a point *h actus* north of, and at angle Z to, the datum point northing N is given by N + (*h Sine* Z) having converted *h* to km. A northing at a point *h actus* south of, and at angle Z to, a given northing N is given by N - (*h Sine* Z) having converted *h* to km. Likewise, E - (*h Cosine* Z), gives an easting *h* actus west of a given co-ordinate E. An easting to the east of the given co-ordinate, is given by E + (*h Cosine* Z).

Appendix 2: Calculating the distances between two given OS grid references in terms of an angled cadastral grid.

Figure A2 represents a grid square aligned at angle z to the meridian (NS line). The grid *tetrans* is at T. P is the point whose relationship to T we wish to know in terms of values for k (*kardo*) and d (*decumanus*). The difference in northings between T and P is n, and the difference in eastings is e.

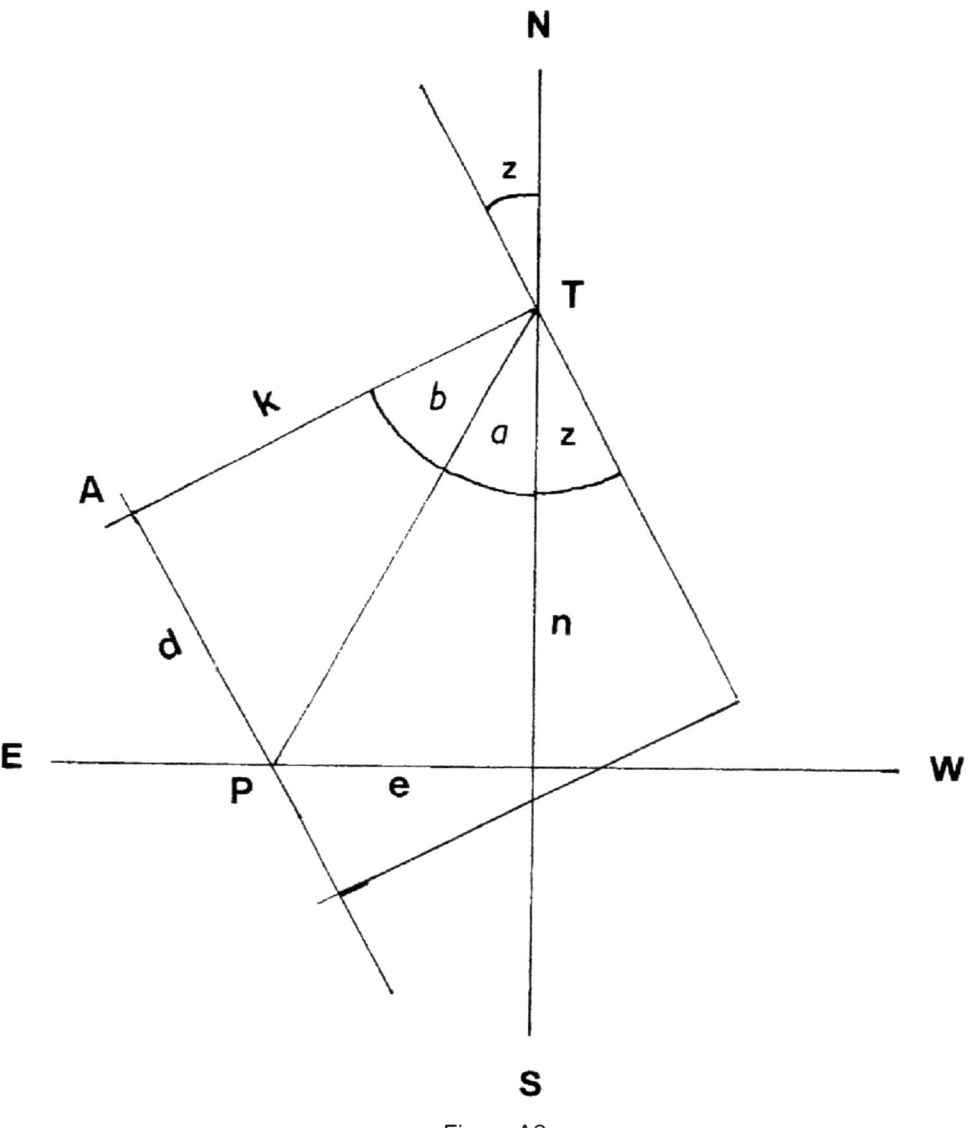

Figure A2

Whence;
1. $TP = \sqrt{(n^2 + e^2)}$ (Pythagoras's theorem)
2. Angles $a + b + z = 90$ (In cadaster B, z = 30.96)
3. Angle $a = Atan\ e/n$
4. Angle $b = 90 - (a + z)$
5. $d = TP\ Sine\ b$
6. $k = TP\ Cosine\ b$

The equations may be arranged in a spreadsheet to give the required values for k and d. The distances are calculated in kilometres and then converted to Roman measure as explained in Appendix 1.

Appendix 3: Linear regression on points along the Carlisle to Reagill Roman road

Location	Eastings	Northings
Reagill	360.85	516.93
Gilshaughlin	357.35	524.32
Brougham	353.80	528.99
White Ox Farm	350.98	531.80
Inglewood Cottage	348.50	543.12
High Hesket	347.73	544.20
Scalesceugh	344.90	549.50
Carleton	342.44	553.10
Gallows Hill	341.04	554.82
Carlisle	339.96	555.90
	Correlation coefficient	0.99
	Slope	0.50
	Slope in degrees	26.63

Appendix 4: Linear regression on the lanes along the Itonfield Street line between Hutton Row and Pow Bank

Location	Eastings	Northings
Pow Bank N.	338.30	550.35
Pow Bank S.	338.52	549.95
Unthank N.	339.12	548.88
Unthank S.	339.77	547.88
Itonfield Street N.	341.10	545.70
Itonfield Street S.	342.25	543.72
Low Grange N.	343.12	542.29
Low Grange S.	343.47	541.80
Morton Mill Road N.	344.49	540.03
Morton Mill Road S.	344.79	539.50
Hutton Row N.	345.28	538.70
Hutton Row S.	345.81	537.72
	Correlation coefficient	1.000
	Slope	0.600
	Slope in degrees	30.96

Appendix 5: Linear regression on the lanes between Middlesceugh and Barrow Mill

Location	Eastings	Northings
Middlesceugh Hall Lane W	340.55	540.83
Braithwaite Hall Lane W1	340.88	540.99
Braithwaite Hall Lane W2	341.08	541.12
Braithwaite Hall Lane mid 1	341.21	541.17
Braithwaite Hall Lane mid 2	341.48	541.30
Braithwaite Hall Lane E 1	341.47	541.35
Braithwaite Hall Lane E 2	341.75	541.53
Low Braithwaite Rd W1	341.80	541.45
Low Braithwaite Rd E1	342.65	542.12
Low Braithwaite Rd W2	343.00	542.17
Low Braithwaite Rd E2	343.28	542.35
Colt Close Rd E	344.09	542.79
Sceughmire Lane W	344.57	543.14
Sceughmire Lane E	344.87	543.30
Petteril Hill Lane W	344.89	543.28
Petteril Hill Lane E	345.50	543.61
	Correlation coefficient	0.999
	Slope	0.571
	Slope in degrees	32.70

Appendix 6: Calculation for the projection of Alignment 2 of the Reagill-Carlisle road

Imagine the road alignment between Reagill and the unknown datum at Carlisle. Logically its length (h) is not known, but it is a hypotenuse, whence the value for e (difference in eastings) is given by *h. Sine* 26.63 . The value for n (difference in northings) is given by *h. Cosine* 25.56. The eastings and northings for the line's end are then found by subtracting e from Reagill's easting and by adding *n* to its northing. The lengths are converted to Roman measure, as shown above. Using a spreadsheet iteratively, that is by trial and error of in-puts for the vale of *h*, an alignment length of 30 Roman miles passed within 30 metres of wall Knowe. The vales for *e* and *n*, when converted to Roman measure, were 28.5 x 20 *actu*s and 57 *actus*, respectively.

Appendix 7: Calculation of the EW dimension of the Cornish peninsula

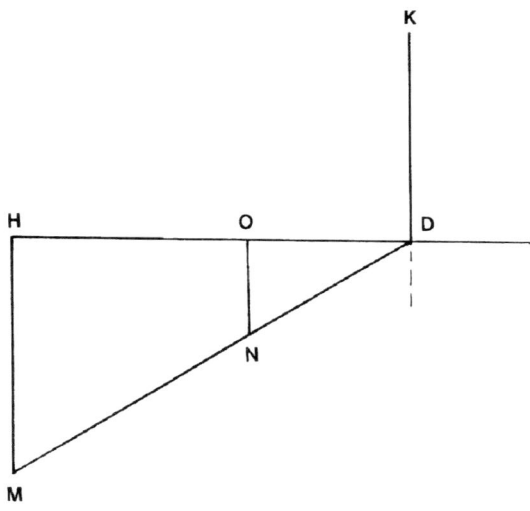

Figure A7

In Figure A7, D is the intersection of the latitude (northing) of *Cantium Prom* with the longitude (easting) of Wall Knowe-Chester. It is a point 200 miles west of *Cantium Prom*. N is the site of *Nemetostatio*, 50 miles E and 30 miles S of D. M is a datum point near St Michael's Mount. DON and DHM are similar triangles whose non-hypotenuse sides are in a whole number ratio, 3:5. The properties of such *rational* right-angled triangles were well understood by the ancients [1]. By Pythagoras's theorem, the hypotenuse of a 3:5 triangle is 5.831 [(25 + 9)]; so in projecting a line from D to N and then on M, each 5.831 miles measured corresponded to five miles further west and three further south. 5.831 miles turns out to be 242.96 actus, which is only 4.8 feet short of 243 *actus* so the line could be readily calibrated with a one *actus* chain. So when point M was reached, the line DM would be 145.774 miles (6,073.92 *actus*). This is 25 x 5.831 miles. Then SH = 75 miles and DH = 125 miles.

Appendix 8: Putative grid-lines of the Roman provincial survey originating at *Cantium Prom*. OS eastings and northings at ten-mile intervals from OS 636.10N 143.30N. (After Ferrar & Richardson 2003)

miles	E	N	miles	E	N	miles	E	N
10	621.31	158.09	110	473.45	305.95	210	325.58	453.82
20	606.53	172.87	120	458.66	320.74	220	310.80	468.60
30	591.74	187.66	130	443.87	335.53	230	296.01	483.39
40	576.95	202.45	140	429.09	350.31	240	281.22	498.18
50	562.17	217.23	150	414.30	365.10	250	266.44	512.96
60	547.38	232.02	160	399.51	379.89	260	251.65	527.75
70	532.59	246.81	170	384.73	394.67	270	236.86	542.54
80	517.81	261.59	180	369.94	409.46	280	222.08	557.32
90	503.02	276.38	190	355.15	424.25	290	207.29	572.11
100	488.23	291.17	200	340.37	439.03	300	192.50	586.90

---

[1] Heath (1921, 81)

Appendix 9: Eastings and northings of *limites* (*quintariae*) of cadaster A

In cadaster A, the *limites* run along the OS grid lines, although their termini are unknown and can only be inferred from the present map evidence. Listed from west to east the calculated values for the *decumani* are: D25W (322.17): D20W (325.71): D15W (329.26): D10W (332.81): D5W (336.36): DM (555.90): D5E (343.46): D10E (347.01): D15E (350.56): D20E (354.11): D25E (357.65). Listed from north to south the calculated values for the *kardines* are: K15N (566.55): K10N (563.00): K5N (559.45: KM (555.90): K5S (552.35). There is not an apparent *kardo* south of Newbiggin Road.

Appendix 10: Possible paradigm for setting out DM (B) from DM (A)

The suggested method, using only *gromae* and measuring chains, is as follows. See Figure A10 a.

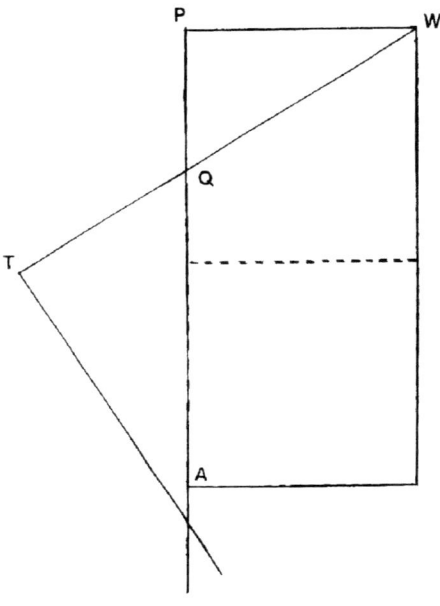

Figure A 10 a

1. Locate the point (P) on DM (A) i.e., 20 *actus* (2,400 feet) west of Wall Knowe (W).
2. Measure 12 *actus* south from P to a point Q, which is thus *Atan* 12/20, or 3/5, S of W from Wall Knowe.
3. WQ gives the line of KM of cadaster B, which is extended southwards and westwards.
4. Calibrate the KM in *actus* west from Wall Knowe. The 40 *actus* (2 *centuriae*) interval is on the spur at the Eden-Caldew confluence (OS 339.45 556.62) where the Wall crosses, point T.
5. A line at right-angles to WT is the DM of cadaster B and cuts the DM of cadaster A just south of *tetrans* A.
6. Continue the DM of cadaster B with constant cross-measurements to the DM of cadaster A (and its prolongation to Mabil Cross). Any point upon DM (B) always relates to DM (A) in the ratio three east to five south, so the course of DM (B) can be pegged out accurately. Because the unitary value on the hypotenuse of the 3:5 triangle is 5.831 (Appendix 7), every 700 feet along DM (B) relates to another 5 *actus* (600 feet) along DM (A). Therefore DM (B) can be set out with the gromae as shown in Figure A10 b, - very simple and very accurate.

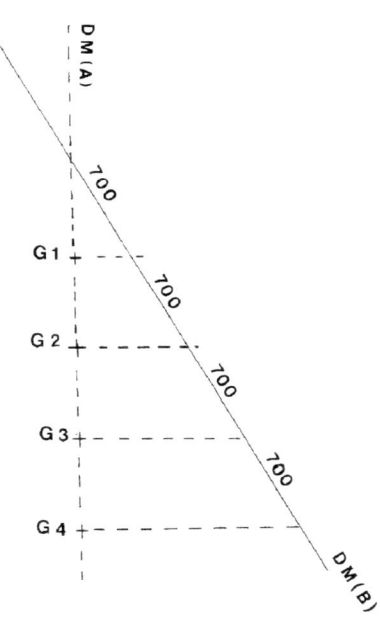

Figure A 10 b

7. Calibrate DM (B) in *centuriae*. This appears to have been started at the rivers' confluence (T) because the Middlesceugh Hall-Barrow Mill *limes*, accurately identified, is 400 *actus* (20 *centuriae*) from that point.
8. With both KM (B) and DM (B) calibrated, the process of setting out the centurial grid may begin.

Appendix 11: Eastings and northings of nodes (*quintariae*) of cadaster B

Because cadaster B is inclined *Atan* 3/5 W of N, the OS grid references for the *quintarial* nodes are given in table format. Table A11 is divided into two parts on account of its size. The first part lists the grid reference of the nodes west of the DM, while the second lists those to the east. All *kardines* are south.

TABLE A11 (PART ONE): OS GRID REFERENCES OF QUINTARIAL NODES IN CADASTER B

	D 20 W		D 15 W		D 10 W		D 5 W	
KM	327.28	549.32	330.32	551.14	333.37	552.97	336.41	554.79
K5	329.10	546.27	332.15	548.10	335.19	549.93	338.24	551.75
K10	330.93	543.23	333.97	545.06	337.02	546.88	340.06	548.71
K15	332.75	540.19	335.80	542.01	338.84	543.84	341.89	545.66
K20	334.58	537.14	337.63	538.97	340.67	540.80	343.71	542.62
K25	336.41	534.10	339.45	535.93	342.49	537.75	345.54	539.58
K30	338.23	531.06	341.28	532.88	344.32	534.71	347.36	536.54
K35	340.06	528.02	343.10	529.84	346.15	531.67	349.19	533.49
K40	341.88	524.97	344.93	526.80	347.97	528.62	351.01	530.45
K45	343.71	521.93	346.75	523.75	349.80	525.58	352.84	527.41
K50	345.53	518.89	348.58	520.71	351.62	522.54	354.67	524.36

TABLE A11 (PART TWO): OS GRID REFERENCES OF QUINTARIAL NODES IN CADASTER B

	DM		D 5 E		D 10 E	
KM	339.45	556.62	342.50	558.45	345.54	560.27
K5	341.28	553.58	344.32	555.40	347.36	557.23
K10	343.10	550.53	346.15	552.36	349.19	554.18
K15	344.93	547.49	347.97	549.32	351.02	551.14
K20	346.76	544.45	349.80	546.27	352.84	548.10
K25	348.58	541.40	351.62	543.23	354.67	545.06
K30	350.41	538.36	353.45	540.19	356.49	542.01
K35	352.23	535.32	355.28	537.14	358.32	538.97
K40	354.06	532.27	357.10	534.10	360.14	535.93
K45	355.88	529.23	358.93	531.06	361.97	532.88
K50	357.71	526.19	360.75	528.01	363.80	529.84

BIBLIOGRAPHY

1. Allan, T. M., 1994: *The Roman Route across the Northern Lake District; Brougham to Moresby,* CNWRS, Lancaster.
2. Anon (undated a): *A plan of roads leading from Carlattan gate to High Gelt Bridge in the parish of Castle Carrock and from thence to the village of Talkin,* (County Record Office, Carlisle, DMh/10/7 Vol. 3, 197).
3. Armstrong, A. M., Mawer, A., Stenton, F. M., Dickens, B., undated: *Placenames of Cumberland,* Vol. 20, Cambridge.
4. Aujac, G., 1987: *Greek Cartography in the Early Roman World,* in Harley and Woodward, 1987.
5. Bellhouse, R. L., & Richardson, G. G. S., 1982: *The Trajanic fort at Kirkbride; the terminus of the Stanegate,* Transactions of the Cumberland and Westmorland Antiquarian and Archaeological Society (2nd Series), lxxxii, 35-50.
6. Bowey, T., 1715: *Thomas Bowey's Map* DX/128/7/21, County Record Office, Carlisle.
7. Bradford, J., 1957: *Ancient Landscapes, London,* cited by Dilke (1971), 136.
8. Breeze, A., 2001: *The Name of the River Petteril,* Transactions of the Cumberland and Westmorland Antiquarian and Archaeological Society (3rd Series), Vol. 1, 195-196.
9. Breeze, D. J. and Dobson B., 2000: *Hadrian's Wall,* Penguin, London.
10. Brook, G. L., 1962: *An Introduction to Old English,* Manchester.
11. Bruce, J. C., 1860: *Handbook to the Roman Wall, XII Edition,* edited, by Sir Ian Richmond, Hindson & Andrew Reid Ltd. Newcastle upon Tyne.
12. Budiansky, S., 1997: *The Nature of Horses,* Weidenfield and Nicholson, London.
13. Campbell, B., 1996: *Shaping the Rural Environment: Surveyors in Ancient Rome,* Journal of Roman Studies, LXXXVI, 74-99.
14. Campbell B. ed., 2000: *The Corpus Agrimensorum Romanorum,* Society for the Promotion of Roman Studies.
15. Caruana, I., and Coulston, J. C., 1987: *A Roman bridge stone from the River Eden, Carlisle,* Transactions of the Cumberland and Westmorland Antiquarian and Archaeological Society (2nd Series), lxxxvii, 43-51.
16. Chevallier, R., 1976: *Roman Roads,* B. T. Batsford, London.
17. Collingwood, R. G., 1937: *Two Roman Mountain Roads,* Transactions of the Cumberland and Westmorland Antiquarian and Archaeological Society (2nd Series) xxxvii, 1-12.
18. Crump, W. B., 1939: *Saltways from the Cheshire Wiches,* Lancashire and Cheshire Antiquarian Society, Vol. LIV, 84-142.
19. Della Corte, M., 1912: III Pompeii. *Continuazione dello scavo dell'Abbondanza, Notische degli Scavi antichita,* cited by Schioler 1994.
20. Dilke, O. A. W., 1971: *The Roman Land Surveyors.* David and Charles, Newton Abbot.
21. Dilke, O. A. W., 1985: *Greek and Roman Maps,* Thames and Hudson, London.
22. Diller, A., 1948: *The Ancient Measurements of the Earth,* Isis Magazine for Oxford University, Vol. XL, 6-9.
23. Dodgson J. McN., 1970: *The Place Names of Cheshire; Part I,* Cambridge.
24. Fabricius, E., 1900: *Bericht uber die Arbeiten der Reichslimeskommission in Jahre 1900,* Archaologischer Anzeiger, Berlin, cited by Schioler 1994.
25. Ferguson, R. S., 1886: *The Beaumont Hoard,* Transactions of the Cumberland and Westmorland Antiquarian and Archaeological Society (1st Series), viii, 373-381.
26. Ferrar, M. J. & Richardson, A., 2003: *The Roman Survey of Britain,* British Archaeological Reports, British Series, 359, Oxford.
27. Forest Proceedings (1217) Chancery 17, cited by Mannix and Whelan 1847.
28. Gosselin, P. F. J. 1883: *Systeme D' Eratosthene,* cited by Harley and Woodward (1987), 153-157.
29. Graham, T. H. B., 1907: *An Old Map of Hayton Manor,* Transactions of the Cumberland and Westmorland Antiquarian and Archaeological Society (2nd Series), vii. 42-51.
30. Graham, T. H. B., 1920: *Carlattan,* Transactions of the Cumberland and Westmorland Antiquarian and Archaeological Society (2nd Series), xx., 19-27.
31. Gray, H. L., 1959: *English Field Systems,* Merlin Press, London.
32. Handford, S. A., 1951: *Caesar: The Conquest of Gaul,* Penguin Classics, London

33. Harley, J. B. & Woodward, D., 1987: *The History of Cartography, vol. 1, Cartography in Prehistoric, Ancient and Mediaeval Europe and the Mediterranean,* University of Chicago.
34. Hardie, C., 1965: *The origin and plan of Roman Florence,* Journal of Roman Studies, Vol. 55, 122-140.
35. Heath, T., 1921: *A History of Greek Mathematics,* Clarendon Press, Oxford.
36. Higham N. J., 1986: Transactions of the Cumberland and Westmorland Antiquarian and Archaeological Society (2nd Series), lxxxvi, 85-100.
37. Hodgkinson and Donald, 1771-1774: *A Map of Cumberland,* County Record Office Carlisle.
38. Hogg, R., 1952: The historic crossings of the River Eden at Stanwix and their associated road system, Transactions of the Cumberland and Westmorland Antiquarian and Archaeological Society (2nd Series), lii, 1131-159.
39. Humphries, A. B., 1993: *Agrarian Change in East Cumberland 1750-1900,* M. Phil. Thesis, University of Lancaster.
40. Hutchinson, W., 1794-97: *A History of the County of Cumberland, Vol. 1, Carlisle.*
41. Lysons, D. & S., 1816: (eds) *Magna Britannia, Vol. IV, Cumberland,* London.
42. McGillivray, H., (undated), *A History of the Parish of Hesket in the Forest,* an unpublished MS, County Record Office, Carlisle.
43. Manning, W. H., 1975: *Economic influences on land use in the military areas of the Highland Zone during the Roman period,* in *The Effect of Man on the Landscape: Highland Zone,* The Council for British Archaeology, Research Rep. No. 11, 112-116.
44. Mannix & Whellan, W., 1847: *History and Gazeteer of Cumberland*
45. Margary, I.D., 1954 - 57: *Roman Roads in Britain,* Phoenix House Ltd., London.
46. Nicholson, J. and Burn, R., 1777: *The History and Antiquities of Westmoreland and Cumberland,* London.
47. Ogden, T. L., 1966: *Cold Harbours and Roman Roads,* Durham University Journal, LIX 13-24.
48. Petrikovits, H. von, 1960: *Das romische Rheinland Archaologische Forschungen seit 1945, Koln und Opladen: Westdeutscher Verlag,* cited by Manning (1975).
49. Piggott, S., 1992: *Wagon, Chariot and Carriage: Symbol and Status, in The History of Transport,* Thames and Hudson, New York, cited by Budiansky S., (1997).
50. Prescott, J. E., 1887: *Registers of Wetheral,* London.
51. Richardson, A., 1982: *Evidence of centuriation in the Inglewood Forest,* Transactions of the Cumberland and Westmorland Antiquarian and Archaeological Society (2nd Series), lxxxii, 67-71.
52. Richardson, A., 1984: *An old road in the Eden valley,* Transactions of the Cumberland and Westmorland Antiquarian and Archaeological Society (2nd Series), lxxxiv, 79-83.
53. Richardson, A., 1986: *Further evidence of centuriation in Cumbria,* Transactions of the Cumberland and Westmorland Antiquarian and Archaeological Society (2nd Series), lxxxvi, 71-78.
54. Richardson, A. & Allan, T. M., 1990: *The Roman road over the Kirkstone Pass: Ambleside to Old Penrith,* Transactions of the Cumberland and Westmorland Antiquarian and Archaeological Society (2nd Series), xc, 105-125.
55. Richardson, A., 2002: *Some probable Roman roads in East Cumbria,* Transactions of the Cumberland and Westmorland Antiquarian and Archaeological Society (3rd Series), ii, 307-309.
56. Richardson, A., 2004 a: *The Romans in the Manchester Area: How They Shaped the Landscape,* published by the author.
57. Richardson, A., 2004 b: *A probable Roman road and possible Roman bridge at Haresceugh,* Transactions of the Cumberland and Westmorland Antiquarian and Archaeological Society (3rd Series), iv, 252-257.
58. Richardson, G. G. S., 1973: *The Roman Tilery, Scalesceugh,* Transactions of the Cumberland and Westmorland Antiquarian and Archaeological Society (2nd Series), lxxiii, 79-89.
59. Richardson, G. G. S, & Richardson, A.., 1980: *A Possible Roman Road in the Kirkstone Pass and Matterdale,* Transactions of the Cumberland and Westmorland Antiquarian and Archaeological Society (2nd Series), lxxx, 160-162.
60. Ross, P., 1920: *The Roman Road north of Low Borrow Bridge, to Brougham Castle, Westmoreland,* Transactions of the Cumberland and Westmorland Antiquarian and Archaeological Society (2nd Series), xx, 1-15.

61. Schioler, T., 1994: *The Pompeii groma in New Light,* Analecta Romana, Instituti Danici, XXII. Rome.
62. Shotter, D. L., 2004: *Romans and Britons in North West England.* CNWRS, Lancaster.
63. Stevenson, L., 1932: *Ptolemy Claudius,* The Geography, New York.
64. Summerson, H., 1991: *Murder at Hutton in the Forest: A study in the government of thirteenth century Cumberland*, Transactions of the Cumberland and Westmorland Antiquarian and Archaeological Society (2nd Series), xci, 59-68.
65. Taylor, M. W., 1892: *The Old Manorial Halls of Cumberland and Westmorland*, Chas Thurnham, Kendal.
66. Welfare, H. & Swan, V., 1995: *Roman Camps in England: The Field Archaeology*, Royal Commission on Historic Monuments, (London, HMSO).
67. Whelan, W., 1860: *History and Topography of Cumberland and Westmorland,* Pontefract.
68. Wilson, P. A., 1976: *Brougham Castle and early communications in the Eden valley,* Transactions of the Cumberland and Westmorland Antiquarian and Archaeological Society (2nd Series), lxxvii, 67-76.

INDEX

A

actus: 12.
actus quadratus: 12.
agrimensores: 11, 18, 19, 24, 32, 39, 48.
Aikbank Common, Calthwaite: 4.
Aiketgate: 7, 16 18, 41.
Aikton: 37, 38, 46.
Aiktongate: 45 47, 49, 50, 54.
Ainstable: 5, 56.
Alexandria: 29.
Allan, T. M. (Martin): 4, 37, 38.
Alston: 50, 51.
Amabil, see Mabil Cross.
Ambleside: 2.
Anglo-Saxons: 3.
Anglo-Saxon Chronicle: 3.
Antonine Wall: 32.
Appleby: 53.
Appleby Street: 4, 39, 52 58.
Armathwaite: 5, 17, 37, 54, 56.
Ashton under Lyne, Lancs.: 55.
Askham, Westmorland: 16, 41, 42, 44.
Aswan, Egypt: 29.
Augury: 13.
Augustus, Roman emperor: 12.
Avignon, France: 13.

B

Barbentone, France: 13.
Barrock Fell: 17.
Barrock Fold (boundary hedge): 17, 41.
Barrow Mill, Southwaite: 13 18, 23, 24, 41, 43, 64, 67.
Beacon Fell, Penrith: 21.
Bellhouse, R.L.: 37.
Berwick upon Tweed: 27.
Birdoswald: 1.
Black Moss Pool, Cotehill: 7.
Blackwell, Carlisle: 36.
Blencarn: 58.
Blencowe: 7, 41, 42.
Boothby, Brampton: 46, 47.
Botchergate, Carlisle: 35, 36.
Bowey, T. (map of): 17, 18, 48.
Bowness on Solway: 1.
Braithwaite Hall: 64.
Brampton: 17, 38, 46, 53, 55, 57.
Brampton Road, Carlisle: 24.
Brampton Street, Carlattan: 5, 8, 37.
Breeze, A.: 19.
Brisco, Carlisle: 47.
Broadfield, Hesket: 5.
Broadwath, Great Corby: 46, 47, 54.
Brockington, R.: 53.
Brougham: 2 4, 8, 15, 21, 22, 51, 57, 63.
Brownrigg, Plumpton: 45.
Bulls Head Farm, Calthwaite: 4.
Burgh Road, Carlisle: 35, 36.
Burnham on Sea, Somerset: 30.

C

Cadasters: 12, 13.
Cadaster A: 19, 23, 36 40, 45, 47, 50, 53, 54, 56, 57.
Cadaster B: 19, 23, 33, 39, 40 42, 44, 45, 47, 48, 50, 57.
Caesar, Julius: 30.
Caldbeck: 7, 8, 47, 49.
Caldew, river: 7, 16, 36, 39, 40, 41, 45.
Calthwaite: 4, 5, 9, 13, 16, 19, 41, 43.
Camp, Roman at Golden Fleece: 47.
Campbell, B.: 11.
Cantium Prom: 25, 30, 31 33, 65.
Carlattan: 5, 37, 56.
Carleton, Carlisle: 21, 22, 63.
Carleton, Penrith: 51.
Carlisle: 2, 7, 8, 14 16, 20 24, 28, 45, 49, 50, 56, 58, 63, 64.
    Cathedral: 20, 37, 38, 40.
    Dean & Chapter (boundary in 1715): 18.
    Roads approaching: 35 37, 39.
Carpentras, France: 13.
Carvoran: 2, 4.
Castle Carrock: 4, 17, 36, 37, 39, 45, 47, 54 57.
Castle Hewen (boundary of): 17, 41.
Castlesteads, Wall fort: 4, 53, 55, 57.
Castrigg: 53, 54.
Catterlen: 19.
Cavallion, France: 13.
Celleron: 42.
centuriae: 11, 12.
Centuriation:
    features of: 11, 12.
    Florence: 19, 23.
    Kent: 12.
    Manchester: 12, 38.
    Old Penrith: 44.
    Rhone Valley: 12, 13.

INDEX

Sussex, 12.
Chateaurenard, France: 13.
Cheshire: 6.
Chester: 24, 25, 30 32, 65, elliptical building at, 32, 33.
Chichester: 25.
Cippi: 12.
Cirencester: 33.
Civil War, British: 48.
Claudius Ptolemy: 27, 29, 30, 32, Geographia: 33.
Cliburn: 21.
Coldharbour place-names: 3.
Collingwood, R.G.: frontispiece, 3, 42.
Colonies, Roman: 12.
Colt Close, Low Braithwaite: 64.
Corbridge: 2, 50.
Corbridgegate: 50, 51.
Cornwall: 30, 31, 65.
Corpus Agrimensorum Romanorum: 11, 32.
Cotehill: 5, 7, 13, 16, 41, 47.
Cotehill Farm, Brampton: 46.
Court Thorn, Hesket: 17, 18, 21.
Crosby Moor: 38.
Cross Fell, Kirkland: 39.
Crossroads House, Brisco: 47.
Culgaith: 58.
Cumbria Sites and Monuments Records: 38, 47.
Cumrew: 54.
Cumwhinton: 41, 45 57.
Cumwhitton: 56, 57.

D

Dacre: 41, 42.
Dacre, Lord: 16.
Dalston: 2, 5, 13, 16, 45, 47, 50.
Danes: 3.
decumanus (maximus): 11, 35, 39.
decumanus maximus of cadaster B: 66.
decumani: 36.
Della Corte, M.: 33.
Devon: 28, 30, 31.
Devonshire Square: 16.
Dilke, O.A.W.: 11, 13, 17, 19, 24.
Donald; see Hodkinson.
Dorset: 27.
Dover: 30.
Durdar, Carlisle: 36, 45 47, 49.

E

Eamont Bridge: 7.
Eamont, river: 7, 8.
East Anglia: 28.
Eden, river: 2, 7, 14, 16, 17, 20, 24, 35, 39, 41, 44, 46, 47, 51, 56, 59.
Edenhall: 51.
Ellen, river: 7, 49.
Ellerbeck Common, Caldbeck: 7.
Ellonby: 7.
English Heritage: 38.
Ennim, Blencowe: 42.
Eratosthenes: 29, 31, 32.
Etruscans: 12.
Etterby Wath: 7, 8, 45.
Ewe Close: 21, 22.
Exeter: 28.

F

Fabricius, E.: 32.
Fairy Bead Lane, Stainton: 42.
Fenton Gate, Hayton: 16, 36, 37.
Ferguson, R.S.: 7, 8, 41, 45.
Ferrar, M.J.: 24, 25, 38, 44.
fford and ford, place-name: 3.
Fiend's Fell: 51.
FitzDuncan, Adam: 38.
Florence: 19, 23.
Formae: 11, 32, 33.
Fosse Way: 15, 33.
Frontinus, Sextus, Julius: 32.

G

Gallowgate, Lunesdale: 58.
Gallows Hill, Carlisle: 21, 22, 63.
Gamblesby: 4, 51.
Gamelsby: 38.
gate place-names, 3.
Gaul: 12, 30.
Gelt, river: 17, 38, 53, 55, 58.
Gilshaughlin Wood, Cliburn: 21, 22, 63.
Glanum, France: 13.
Golden Fleece: 47.
Gosforth: 3.
Grampians: 1.
Great Corby: 17, 45, 46, 54, 56, 57.
Great Easby, Brampton: 46.

INDEX

Great Orton: 36, 37.
Great Salkeld: 44.
Great Strickland: 41, 42.
Greece: 12.
Greek surveying: 12, 33, town plan 35.
Green Lane, Pow Bank: 5, 6, 20, 46, 49.
Greenrigg, Caldbeck: 7.
Greenwich: 27.
Greystoke: 38.
groma: 11, 32, 33.
Gyrgwath: 7.

H

Hadrian's Wall: 1, 2, 4, 14, 15, 20, 24, 32, 35, 40, 45, 46, 47, 49, 57, 58, 59.
Hall's Tenement, Carlattan: 37.
Haltcliffe: 7.
Harbour, place-name: 3.
Harbour Wood, Wetheral: 47.
Haresceugh: 52, 56.
Hartington Place, Carlisle: 36.
Hartside Cross: 50, 51, 52, 53, 56, 57.
Hawksdale, Dalston: 45, 46, 47, 49.
Hayton: 5, 16, 17, 19, 36, 38, 45, 46.
Hayton Gate: 46.
Heads Nook: 5, 47.
Hee Street at Cotehill: 5, 7, 8, 13, 15 17, 41.
Helton, Westmorland: 44.
Henry II, King: 7.
Herodotus: 29.
Hesket: 2, 5, 13, 16, 17, 22.
Hesket Newmarket: 5, 7, 49, 63.
Hexham: 50.
High Hesket: 15 17, 21, 22, 47, 48.
High Northsceugh: 14, 41.
High Street: 2, 42.
Hodkinson & Donald's map: 5, 15, 46, 49.
Hoghouse Hill, Newbiggin: 42.
Holme Coultram (records): 45.
Honiton, Devon: 28.
Hornsbygate: 56.
Horses: 1.
How Street, Hayton: 5, 8, 16, 17, 24, 38, 39, 46, 54.
Howeknowe Pike, Westmorland: 21, 22.
Hutton in the Forest: 6, 16.
Hutton Row: 5, 6, 13, 16, 20, 43, 63.
Hutton Sceugh, Hesket Newmarket: 14.

I

Ilchester, Somerset: 25,
Inglewood:
   Cottage, Hesket: 22, 63.
   Forest, 2, 5, 6, 8, 15, 16, 18, 38, 48,
   Serjeanties: 15, 42.
Irthing, river: 17, 46.
Italy: 12.
Itonfield Street: 5, 6, 8, 13, 14 21, 23, 24, 28, 40, 43, 63.
Ivegill: 5.

K

kardo (maximus): 11, 12, 35.
kardines: 36, 38.
Kent: 30.
Kenwathen: 7.
Keswick: 2, 4.
Kirkbampton: 38, 39.
Kirkbride: 2, 4, 36 39, 47.
Kirkby Thore: 2, 4.
   possible cadaster at, 58.
Kirkland: 39.
Kirkstone Pass: 4.

L

Lanercost Bridge: 45, 46, 57.
Langwathby: 51.
Latitude: 12, 23, 28, 31.
Lazonby: 41, 44, 45.
Lessonhall: 36, 37.
Lincoln: 25.
Linear regression: 22, 23, 63, 64.
Little Bampton: 38.
Little Orton: 38.
Little Strickland: 42.
London: 25.
Long Dyke, Castle Carrock: 53, 55.
Long Dyke Farm, Castle Carrock: 53.
Longitude, see meridian,
   mid longitude: 30, 31, 33.
Long Marton: 4, 58.
Low Borrowbridge: 21, 22, 24, 58.
Low Braithwaite: 5, 6, 42, 43, 63, 64.
Low Gelt Bridge: 46, 53, 55.
Low Grange, Low Braithwaite: 5, 6, 63.
Low Street, Hesket: 5.

INDEX

Low Street, Plumpton: 5, 7, 45.
Low Whinnow 46.
Low Wood Beck, Reagill: 21.
Lune valley, possible cadaster: 58.
Lyne Beck, Calthwaite: 6.
Lysons, D. & S.: 5.
Lytle Street, Hesket: 5.

M

Mabil Cross, or Mabel Cross: 7, 38, 39, 48.
Magna via, place-name, 3.
Maiden Way: 2.
Manchester: 32, 38, 55.
Manning, W. H.: 1, 2.
Maps:
   projections, Greek: 26, 27.
    Roman Britain: 28.
Maryport: 2, 4.
Matterdale: 4.
Mealsgate: 2.
Melandra, Derbys.: 55.
Melmerby: 4.
Meridian: 12, 21, 23, 28, 30, 36.
Middlesceugh: 13 18, 23, 24, 40 43, 64, 67.
Middleton, Lunesdale: 58.
Milburn: 4, 58.
Millhouse, Hesket Newmarket: 7.
Morland: 41, 42.
Morton Mill Road, Calthwaite: 5, 6, 9, 63.
Moscow Farm, Alston: 50.
Mydle Sceuth Yate: 16.

N

Nemetostatio: 30, 31, 65.
Newbiggin Hall, Carlisle: 45, 46.
Newbiggin Road, Carlisle: 36, 38, 39, 45 47, 57, 66.
Newbiggin, Stainton: 42.
Nile, river: 29.
Norfolk: 28, *limites* in: 28.
Norman Conquest: 3, 6, 15.
North Sceugh: 41.
North Tawton, Devon, see Nemestatio.

O

Old Carlisle: 2, 8.
Old King's Road (Caldbeck): 7, 49.
Old Penrith: 2, 4, 21, 43.

Orange, France: 12.
Orchard House, Calthwaite: 41.
Ordnance Survey: 27, 33, 38.
Orton Scar, Westmorland: 21.
Oughterby: 36 38.
Ousby: 4.

P

Pallet Hill: 7, 42.
Papcastle: 2, 4, 6.
Park End, Caldbeck: 7.
Park Fauld, Durdar: 45, 46.
Peddar's Way, Norfolk: 28.
Pennines: 1.
Penrith: 3, 7, 8, 20, 45, 50, 52, 57.
Perch: 19.
Pertica: 19.
Petteril Hill Lane, Southwaite: 64.
Petteril, river: 13, (name of) 19, 46.
Piccadilly, Manchester: 32.
Pliny: 29.
Plumpton: 5, 44.
Plumpton Street: 5.
Pompeii: 33.
Poole, Dorset: 27.
Posidonius: 29.
Pow Bank: 5, 16, 20, 63.
Ptolemy; see Claudius Ptolemy.
Pythagoras: 30, 39.
Pytheas of Marseilles: 29, 30.

Q

Quintarius: 12, 36, 46, 47, 55.
   in cadaster A: 66.
   in cadaster B: 67.

R

Raughton Head: 16.
Raven Beck, Renwick: 52, 55.
Raven Bridge, Renwick: 52, 53.
Reagill: 15, 21 24, 35, 40, 63, 64.
Reformation: 48.
Renwick: 4, 51 54, 56, 57.
Rhone valley, France: 12, 13.
Richardson, G. G. S. (George): 4, 16, 19, 41, 56.
Ricker Gill, Haresceugh: 52, 53, 56.
Ringate or Ring Gate, Castle Carrock: 56.

INDEX

Roads: Roman,
  authentic, with termini in alphabetical order.
  Aikton-Dalston: see Aiktongate.
  Ambleside Old Penrith: 4.
  Appleby-Brampton; see Appleby Street.
  Armathwaite-Castle Carrock; see Street to Armathwaite.
  Brougham-Ambleside; see High Street.
  Brougham-Maryport: 4.
  Brougham Stainmore: 53, 58.
  Carlisle-Kirkbride, see Stanegate.
  Carlisle-Longtown: 35.
  Carlisle-Low Borrowbridge: 15, 20 24, 28, 35, 40, 64.
  Carlisle-Papcastle: 2, 6, 35, 47.
  Carlisle Penrith (Brougham): 3, 7, 15, 16, 17, 23, 35, 46, 47, 51,
  Carvoran-Kirkby Thore; see Maiden Way.
  Castlesteads-Castrigg: see Appleby Street.
  Corbridge-Kirkbride; see Stanegate,
  Corbridge-Brougham, see Corbridgegate.
  Dalston-Lanercost; see Aiktongate.
  Exeter Honiton, Devon: 28.
  Hartside-Renwick,
  Old Penrith-Greystoke Moor Troutbeck, 42.
  Kirkbride-Old Carlisle: 2.
  Manchester-Melandra: 55.
  features of, 3.
Roman invasion of Britain: 30.
Romney Marsh, Kent: 30.
Ross, P.: 21.
Roundthwaite, Westmorland: 21, 22.
Rowland Beck: 7.
Ruckcroft: 42.
Rylands Farm, Warnell: 49.

S

Saint Bee's Head: 1.
Saint Michael's Mount, Cornwall: 30, 31, 65.
Saint Paulinus: 39.
Saint Remy, France: 13.
Salisbury Plain: 32.
Salter Lonning, Hesket Newmarket: 7.
Saltus: 42.
Saughtreegate: 5, 45, 53 57.
Scales Hall, Low Braithwaite: 13.
Scalesceugh: 15, 17, 21, 63.
  Roman tilery: 47.
Scatterbeck, Great Salkeld: 44.
Sceughmire Lane, Low Braithwaite: 64,
Scilly Isles: 27.
Scotby: 16, 36, 37.
Scotland: 1, 58.
Scotland Road, Carlisle: 35.
Selah, Haresceugh: 52.
Shap: 42, 59.
Shotter, D.: 1.
Skelton: 2, 13, 14, 16, 40, 42.
Sockbridge: 44.
Sockbridge Hall: frontispiece, 42.
Solway Firth: 1, 2, 8.
South Foreland, Dover: 30.
Southwaite: 16, 41.
Sowerby: 7.
Sowerby Row: 16, 41, 42.
Sparket, near Dacre: 42.
Spreadsheets:
  to define OS grid references with an angled grid: 20, 61.
  to determine agrimensorial co-ordinates from a known OS datum point, 20, 62.
Sprunston: 16.
stade: 29.
Stainton: 41, 42.
Stane Street, Sussex: 25.
Stanegate: 1, 2, 36, 39, 46.
Stanwix, Carlisle: 21, 24.
Strabo: 30.
Street from/to Armathwaite: 5, 17, 37, 54, 56, 57.
Street at Castle Carrock: 5.
Street at Hesket Newmarket: 49.
Street at Plumpton: 5.
Street at Reagill: 15, 21.
Street Close, Hesket: 5.
Street Dale at Castle Carrock: 5.
Street Field at Castle Carrock: 5.
Street Field, Low Braithwaite: 5, 24.
Street Field, Saughtreegate: 5.
Street Head, Low Braithwaite: 5, 6.
Street place-names: 3, 5.
Street Head, Hesket Newmarket: 5, 7.
Street House, Ainstable: 5.
Street House, Hayton: 5.
Street House, Reagill: 21.